Rage

Ed Adams

a firstelement production

First published in Great Britain in 2022 by firstelement
Copyright © 2022 Ed Adams
Directed by thesixtwenty

10 9 8 7 6 5 4 3 2 1

A CIP catalogue record for this book is available from the British
Library.

ISBN 13: 978-1-913818-26-5
eBook ISBN: 978-1-913818-27-2

Printed and bound in Great Britain by Ingram Spark

rashbre
an imprint of firstelement.co.uk
rashbre@mac.com

ed-adams.net

Thanks

A big thank you for the tolerance and bemused support from all of those around me. To those who know when it is time to say, "step away from the keyboard!" and to those who don't.

To Julie for an understanding that only comes with really knowing.

To Carol and Johnny for extensive coaching particularly on flying hot, fast aircraft.

To Steve for the ongoing support of artifacts.

To thesixtwenty.co.uk for direction.

To the NaNoWriMo gang for the continued inspiration and encouragement.

To Topsham, for being lovely.

To the edge-walkers. They know who they are.

And, of course, thanks to the extensive support via the random scribbles of rashbre via
http://rashbre2.blogspot.com
and its cast of amazing and varied readers whether human, twittery, smoky, artistic, cool kats, photographic, dramatic, musical, anagrammed, globalized, or maxed.

Not forgetting the cast of characters involved in producing this; they all have virtual lives of their own.

And of course, to you, dear reader, for at least 'giving it a go'.

Books by Ed Adams include:

Triangle Trilogy		About
1	The Triangle	Dirty money? Here's how to clean it
2	The Square	Weapons of Mass Destruction – don't let them get on your nerves
3	The Circle	The desert is no place to get lost
4	The Ox Stunner	The Triangle Trilogy – thick enough to stun an ox
		(all feature Jake, Bigsy, Clare, Chuck Manners)
Archangel Collection		
1	Archangel	Sometimes I am necessary
2	Raven	An eye that sees all between darkness and light
3	Card Game	Throwing oil on a troubled market
4	Magazine Clip	the above three in one heavy book.
5	Play On, Christina Nott	Christina Nott, on Tour for the FSB
6	Corrupt	Trouble at the House
7	Sleaze	Autos, Politics, Gstaad
		(all feature Jake, Bigsy, Clare, Chuck Manners)
Big Science Textbook		
1	Coin	Get rich quick with Cybercash – just don't tell GCHQ
2	An Unstable System	Creating the right kind of mind
3	The Watcher	We don't need no personal saviours here
4	Jump	Some kind of future
5	Pulse	Want more? Just stay away from the edge
6	Rage	Dealt from a darkened room
Blade's Edge Trilogy		
1	Edge	World end climate collapse and sham discovered during magnetite mining from Jupiter's moon Ganymede.
2	Edge Blue	Earth's endgame, unless…
3	Edge Red	An artificially intelligent outcome, unless…
4	Edge of Forever	Edge Trilogy

About Ed Adams Novels:

Triangle Trilogy		About
1	Triangle	Money laundering
2	Square	A viral nerve agent being shipped by terrorists and WMDs
3	Circle	In the Arizona deserts, with the Navajo; about missiles stolen from storage.
4	Ox Stunner	the above three in one heavy book.
		(all feature Jake, Bigsy, Clare, Chuck Manners)
Archangel Collection		
1	Archangel	Biographical adventures of Russian trained Archangel, who, as Christina Nott, threads her way through other Triangle novels.
2	Raven	Big business gone bad and being a freemason won't absolve you
3	Card Game	Raven Pt 2 – Russian oligarchs attempt to take control
4	Magazine Clip	the above three in one heavy book.
5	Play On, Christina Nott	Christina Nott, on Tour for the FSB
6	Corrupt	Parliamentary corruption
7	Sleaze	Autos, Politics, Gstaad
		(all feature Christina Nott, Jake, Bigsy, Clare, Chuck Manners)
Big Science Textbook		
1	Coin	Cyber cash manipulation by the Russian state.
2	An Unstable System	Creating the right kind of mind
3	Jump	Some kind of future
4	The Watcher	From the Big Bang to the almost Almighty Whimper
5	Pulse	Sci-Fi dystopian blood management with nano-bots
6	Rage	A madman's war
Blade's Edge Trilogy		
1	Edge	World end climate collapse and sham discovered during magnetite mining from Jupiter's moon Ganymede.
2	Edge Blue	Endgame, for Earth – unless?
3	Edge Red	Museum Earth – unless?
4	Edge of Forever	Edge Trilogy

Ed Adams Novels: Links

Triangle Trilogy		Link:	Read?
1	Triangle	https://amzn.to/3c6zRMu	
2	Square	https://amzn.to/3sEiKYx	
3	Circle	https://amzn.to/3qLavYZ	
4	Ox Stunner	https://amzn.to/3sHxlgh	
Archangel Collection			
1	Archangel	https://amzn.to/2Y9nB5K	
2	Raven	https://amzn.to/2MiGVe6	
3	Raven's Card	https://amzn.to/2Y8HLgs	
4	Magazine Clip	https://amzn.to/3pbBJYn	
5	Play On, Christina Nott	https://amzn.to/2MbkuHl	
6	Corrupt	https://amzn.to/2M0HnOw	
7	Sleaze	https://amzn.to/3sE3UDt	
8	An Unstable System	https://amzn.to/2PRJciF	
Big Science Textbook			
1	Coin	https://amzn.to/3o82wmS	
2	An Unstable System	https://amzn.to/2PRJciF	
3	Jump	https://amzn.to/3kTFWjg	
4	The Watcher	https://amzn.to/3sCzK3h	
5	Pulse	https://amzn.to/3qQlBvL	
6	Rage		
Edge of forever Trilogy			
1	Edge	https://amzn.to/2KDmYOW	
2	Edge Blue	https://amzn.to/2Kyq9au	
3	Edge Red	https://amzn.to/2KzJwjz	
4	Edge of Forever	https://amzn.to/3c57Ghj	

PART ONE

Author's Note

This story links with others but can be read alone. The strongest links are to Pulse, Jump, Play On Christina Nott and distantly to Edge.

The Circle Game

Yesterday a child came out to wander
Caught a dragonfly inside a jar
Fearful when the sky was full of thunder
And tearful at the falling of a star

And the seasons, they go round and round
And the painted ponies go up and down
We're captive on the carousel of time
We can't return, we can only look
Behind, from where we came
And go round and round and round, in the circle game

16 springs and 16 summers gone now
Cartwheels turn to car wheels through the town
And they tell him, "Take your time, it won't be long now
'til you drag your feet to slow the circles down"

So, the years spin by and now the boy is 20
Though his dreams have lost some grandeur coming true
There'll be new dreams, maybe better dreams, and plenty
Before the last revolving year is through

And the seasons, they go round and round
And the painted ponies go up and down
We're captive on the carousel of time
We can't return, we can only look
Behind, from where we came
And go round and round and round, in the circle game
And go round and round and round, in the circle game

Joni Mitchell

Preface

Farallon, Limantour, Tomales and Drake are Watchers in a singular metaverse learning how to travel the timeline and now to become Persona in another human Presence.

Scrive, Charlie and Chantel exist in the near future, after the ravages of a Pandemic and the so-named Klima Wars.

A madman starts a war and equilibrium is lost.

The dealer sits in his darkened room.

So, It Begins

Waken

I wake up in a hotel room. It's well provisioned, at what I'd say was early 21st century business class. Maple finish doors. On the walls, ironic pictures of unrecognisable landmarks inhabited by quirky people. Nothing free-standing which could easily be put into travel luggage. Instagram friendly.

I could hear someone else in the shower. My awareness was returning slowly, like the hotel kettle filling from a slow tap. Closer inspection and I could see a cluster of three black marks each about the size of a coffee mug ring on the lower section of the entrance door. Then further up, another three clustered black marks. Scorch marks or the points on a tree bark where branches would have hung.

I remembered the paradox, I was Farallon. A Watcher who became a Wakener, but then, at Limantour's behest, I was ported into a human named Scrive.

It had been trippy, being associated with a specific human. My host had been jacked on tropus and nanobot engineering and, I'm told, for a human possessed extremely fast thought and reflex.

Yeah, right, but not fast enough to avoid being zapped by a Trigax Rail Gun in the back streets of London. I assumed that was how I came to be here now, in this hotel room, listening to someone else showering while I appeared to still possess the restored body of Scrive.

The door to the shower bathroom opened and the toned body of Limantour stepped into the room, oblivious to her lack of clothing.

"Hey, Farallon, I said it'd be wild," she began. As she turned, I noticed three marks on her dark skin, like the marks on the door. It appeared to be the residual burn marks from a Trigax.

She wrapped herself in a hotel towel.

"I'd forgotten you were in here, let alone human sensibilities," she said, "We are still operating as Wakeners. Just like I described when we sat on the racetrack in Norway. I'm still Chantel.

I still had some of my Watcher powers, carried forward into my guise as a Wakener. Limantour - the mistress of chaos - had lectured me about my transition from a Watcher into a Wakener. I replayed the key facts in my mind, whilst she rapidly assembled an outfit.

"You'll be able to act now, and not only that, but you'll also carry some knowledge of the future. Your mind has been loaded with the next 300 years of developments, but I sense we've been given an edit."

"And - You'll be linked into a specific human. Scrive in your case. Humans operate slowly, so you'll have to get used to that, although you can help them at our normal speed of thought and knowledge. You'll need to get used to travel at a human rate. No hops to another position on the earth. And you'll need to take care of your human. They are not immortal like us, and our persistence is interrupted if they are killed. You'll still be able to get back to the Wakener dimension though."

That was it. Persistence interrupted. My human, Scrive, and I guessed Limantour's human named Chantel had been killed. Our persistence had been interrupted. We were now into uncharted territory.

I looked from the window. A street scene, but with Cyrillic writing. A small tobacconist shop opposite and a parade of small hipster cafes. There's a kind of green sheen over everything, which I realise is being cast by the sky, more green than blue, like something from the Northern Lights.

Then I remembered that Drake and Tomales had also experienced the same transition with their Personas entering the Presence of others, but there was no hint that they were around here. I guess they are survivors.

Limantour grins. She is now wearing a bright green zebra patterned dress, "And remember: You'll need to resist some of the human emotional traits. It can be like a massive sensory overload when you start."

"Yes, that explains a few things," I reply, feeling shaken at Limantour's 'grand reveal' a few moments earlier.

"Where's the dress from?" I ask

"Kapsula, one of the nearby shops. I was here before you. It gave me a chance to slip out to get a few things. Good selection."

"But I think your name changed to Chantel - a so-called London socialite?"

"Mad-cap socialite," replied the Mistress of Chaos.

"Of course you are," I thought.

"I was wrong about one thing," answered Limantour, "Our Wakener back-channels still function. We can still communicate to one another silently. So, I can still read your thoughts."

I realised that Limantour had not spoken the reply. We still had that direct affinity.

"Can we reach Tomales and Drake," I asked, "Or should I say Charlie and Nathan?"

"I don't know," answers Limantour, "I can't seem to find either of them. I suppose they could still be okay in their first Presences?"

"The thing is, Scrive works so much better when he's around Charlie," I explain.

"Maybe it's a range thing?" asked Limantour, "I don't know how far our back-channels reach. You've realised this isn't London?"

I looked at the Hilton hotel signage in the room. Cyrillic. I could still read it though, my Watcher powers seemed to be intact. Limantour was reaching for the TV remote

"Whoa," I said.

"Shevchenkivs'kyi district, Kyiv" I uttered.

The TV started, in English. It seemed to know about us both too. Scrive Mallinson and Chantal le Strang.

"It's great that Chantal has multiple names, too, also

Daisy Stone!" said Limantour.

I was more blown away by the fact we were in Kyiv, Ukraine and the date showing on the television.

"We are two days from the start of the first Klima War," I look towards Limantour, then adding, "Remember those big history dates? 4-July-1776 American Independence, 1066 Battle of Hastings, 1914 Start of Great War, 1939 World War II starts, 8-May-1845 Victory in Europe, 22-2-22 Start of First Klima War."

"I always thought they moved the official start to 22-2-22 to make it easy to remember" says Limantour, "It started on 20-02-22."

"And today is the 19th. Well, we are right at the start of it, anyway," I say to Limantour, "Tell me it's not more of your crazy chaos?"

"No - I really don't know about any of this,"

"And how will we extricate ourselves?"

"Well, you're some kind of fly-boy marine and I'm a fashion statement. How hard can it be? We'd better use our human names from now on."

Mikoyan-Gurevich

We look at a map. It was one that Chantal obtained from the Concierge.

I could see the shopping districts prominently displayed but was looking for the airport.

"Why the airport? Are we leaving?" asked Chantal.

"Yes. Put it like this. If we stay another couple of days then the prelude to the Klima Wars is going to kick off from right here. Today, we can still get out, but I think we'll need to use some stealth."

I looked around and with a combination of Scrive's skills, soon located the Vasylkiv Air Base, home to the 40th Tactical Aviation Brigade.

"These guys fly Mikoyan-Gurevich MiG-25PD aircraft. That's a kind of interceptor, but nowadays is mainly used for reconnaissance. The good news is they are fast and can fly high. The bad news is that they are from the 1980s, so around 40 years old."

"Just tell me why we need to know about them?" asks

Chantel.

"Have you ever been in a twin seater jet fighter?" I ask, "Only, it is about to become our getaway vehicle."

I was secretly amazed that riding on Scrive's impulses we were about to break into a military base to steal a jet fighter.

"My first," says Chantal, "And how fast will we go?"

"These things fly at Mach 2. It's fast," I explain.

We decide to get a taxi to the air base. Chantal would have a story about a meeting, and that I was driving her. It was one of those times when I thought we'd need more proof points, but Chantal had also visited a couple of other shops and found a tattoo parlour which didn't mind making various pass-cards.

Chantal seems to have a natural affinity for street culture and so we were soon equipped with two scuffed driving licences, our original Dutch passports and even an invitation to the air base.

Chantal was the official visitor and I was to be her assistant. We used an American Express card to purchase bolt cutters and a large carryall, from the same shopping area where Chantal had shopped for fashion clothing. I simply added to Scrive's collection of black tee-shirts, jackets, and jeans.

"Okay, let's hit it then," says Chantal, as we jumped into a taxi and asked for the way to the airbase. By my reckoning, it would be tomorrow that Putin would make his first attack on Ukraine, after which all cross-border travel would cease.

Airbase

The road to the airbase was quiet, and the taxi pulled into a lay-by close to the main entrance.

"Do you want to go inside, because I don't have a pass?" asks the driver.

"You can drop us here,"

I am now wearing an almost entirely black outfit, and the driver looks confused, as if he knows we are up to no good.

We are outside of the taxi, which is already pulling away. The driver has dropped us next to a small industrial-looking shop that seems to sell tyres and batteries. Along the road a little way is a filling station. Between the two buildings is a row of trees and a lightweight wire fence.

"Bolt cutters," I say and we are soon through the wire fence and on military property. This is where Scrive really wants to own the moment. We run forward and I can see a row of light blue aircraft, parked on an apron which leads to the runway.

"That's the MiG," I say to Chantel, pointing at a large grey plane with stars painted on its wings.

"It's huge!" she replies, I was expecting a sports car plane."

"Yes, they look bigger in real life, don't they!" I secretly thought it looked as big as a second world war bomber.

I gesture to one of the smaller prettier planes painted in a pastel blue camouflage colour. "How about one of these?" I suggest to Chantal.

"Yes!' she jumps in the air as a sign of appreciation.

There's no-one around this part of the compound. I see some G-suits hanging up and grab two, a large for me and a small female for Chantal. We wriggle into the suits and I show Chantal where to stow her documentation and the various plugs which need to be connected into the aircraft.

Then I wheel a short ladder to the nearest plane. The two seats are in-line. Chantal climbs into the rear one and I check as she plugs in and I then climb into the front.

Chantal looks at the plane. "It looks good from afar, but when you get up close these rivets look rusty. Are you sure it is alright?"

I also notice the poor state of maintenance of the plane but reckon that the Russians have supplied them to Ukraine to continue to work even in a somewhat run-down condition. It seems at odds with the so-called 'glass cockpit' display which has replaced all the conventional dials inside. I mildly wonder about the connector from the plane to the display.

I check Chantal is plugged in and then flick switches to start up the plane. Scrive has obviously flown this type of plane before. It's a Sukhoi-27, which is still a huge beast of an air superiority plane with an almost 2,000-mile range. I feel as if I'm on autopilot. With Scrive's motor skills, I realise I'm literally on autopilot.

We'll only need to fly around 500 miles to be out of Ukranian airspace and into Poland. My main worry is about being shot down, either after take-off or on the approach to Poland. I try to remember the interception protocol. Something to do with rocking wings after interception. I'll need to look distressed. In fact, I will be distressed. Very distressed.

Flight

I power the plane along to the runway and could hear something in the headset about identification. I explained we had been scrambled for an intercept and the control tower let me pass, seemingly surprised by the news.

"Is it happening?" asks the tower, "Are they coming?"

Then I manoeuvre with Scrive's capable piloting and am ready for take-off. I'm surprised by the noise as the twin turbofan bypass engines kick in producing the take-off thrust in seconds. The sound drowns out everything. I instinctively adjust the green headphones covering my ears. There's a moment of hollow sound and then the jet engines seem to have been silenced. Chantal's voice is in my ear.

"Wow, you have to fiddle with these headphones to get the noise to quieten. I can still feel the vibration though."

Everything is happening fast and Scrive's instinctive piloting puts us into the air and on a climb that seems to go on forever. I realise we are moving to a safe altitude, even higher than commercial airliners.

I say safe, but only until we approach the Polish border, where I would need all my best powers of diplomacy to effect entry to Polish airspace and a landing.

I work out the timings. Mach 1.5 means we would only need around half an hour in the air to reach Poland. Sure enough, before I'd really had time to think, I receive English language 'Identify' questions from Poland. They were treating us as an unidentified incoming plane. They used a war designation as part of the identification and ask for my serial number. It's the tag on the tail of the plane and different from the usual commercial designation.

It's also stencilled inside the cockpit, so I supply the number, also saying we have been sent over as part of an emergency task force.

Then I notice two NATO F-15 planes running intercept. I waggle my wings to indicate I would comply with instructions and slow right down to around 500 knots. They both overshoot and then I see one take position left and above and the other one disappears, so I know it is behind me.

Mercifully, no radar locks have started pinging, and I realise they are treating me as a curiosity rather than as a threat, although I know they each have the speed, manoeuvrability, and firepower to end everything if things slide sideways.

The forward plane takes control and signals for me to follow. I know this protocol and assume we are going to a suitable airstrip.

My radar shows we are by now just outside of Kraków. The forward F-15 pulls away and I can see it is indicating for me to land on a military airstrip far below. I fly over the runway once to check its length and condition and then turn to make a final approach. The F-15s give me airspace for the manoeuvre and I can hear their chatter to the ground, explaining that they had found me as a stray incoming.

"It's true, then," says the tower, "The invasion of Luhansk and Donetsk has started. We should expect others."

Now it's time for my landing and I bring the slippery SU-27 plane down, in the process using almost all the runway.

The tower speaks to me saying 'use the airbrake' and 'fire the chutes', but I sense this is outside of Scrive's knowledge.

As we almost reach the end of the runway, I feel a judder and realise that Scrive has punched the drag chute control. Behind me, through the headphones, I can hear Chantal being sick.

"I'm sorry, most of it is in the plane"

"Never a dull moment," I state.

"I was wondering about my new look as we came in for that landing. It was a good idea to wear the green outfit. Now it matches my complexion." Chantal is back on form.

I manoeuvre the plane around as a circus of small trucks approach. I decide a white flag could be useful, but instead must raise my hands and put them on my head. I glance behind me and can see that Chantal has done similar.

As we climb out of the plane, we realise we are now prisoners of Poland, in a stolen Soviet-built plane belonging to the Ukrainians. It will take some explaining, even with our Dutch passports.

Volvo

They are speaking in English. It's the crew from one of the F-15s. They are British.

"What on earth?" asks one. They can see our Ukranian flight suits. He wears a pistol holster and his friend has a Beretta pistol in his hand.

I start the explanation. "We were tasked to leave Kyiv with news of the invasion. Putin is moving into attack mode and has a 40-kilometre convoy bound for Kyiv." I struggle to remember more from the stories of the time when the conflict started.

"By the end of the week, Putin will be targeting major infrastructure, even power plants."

Chantal adds, "He is playing poker, not chess. He is bluffing that no-one will want to stop him for fear of starting World War III."

"Gentleman, Lady, we need to take you to the Commanding Officer of the base,"

I wonder how we will be able to get out of this. They put

us into the back of a military Land Cruiser and then there's about ten minutes of conversation between the NATO pilots and the various ground crew, who are all still outside. I can see a couple of them wearing yellow and blue ribbons for Ukraine.

Then most of the mixed convoy of trucks roll off. We wait another five minutes and then they start to ferry us across the airstrip. I'm surprised to see the two Brits travelling in the back of our vehicle.

"Look, you'd better get out of those flight suits," says one of the Brits, "I assume you have other clothes underneath?" He looks at Chantal as he says this.

I can see Chantal is still wearing her green zebra-print and I'm in my new black tee-shirt and black jeans combo from Kapsula.

We are soon back dressed as civilians and then one of the Brits bangs on the panel of the Land Cruiser. The vehicle stops and he gestures for us to disembark.

We stand on the outskirts of the airstrip. I wonder if we are to be shot like in a terrible gangland movie.

The first Brit speaks, "Look, we've been following the news today. What they are doing to your country is terrible. I don't know why you are here, or what you are trying to do, but we're going to bid you 'God speed' to achieve it. There's an exit from the 'strip over there, and you should see a few cars parked about a kilometre along the road, to your left. There's a blue Volvo among them - KR94038."

He hands me a car key.

"Use the car. Drive to Krakow train station, park in the car park at the mall and leave the keys in the glove box. Then, take a train to somewhere, or hire or steal something. We'll be along in two hours to collect the car. Be long gone."

He looks at us both, shakes our hands and then salutes.

"I heard President Volodymyr Zelensky when he said, 'I need ammunition, not a ride.' I think now is a good time for you also to decide."

We make our way out of the airstrip through a small hole in the fence. Chantal was shaking, but I realise this must all be in day's work for Scrive.

Do Not Trespass

We walk along the airport perimeter road. There are multilingual warnings about not trespassing. Then we arrive at the lay-by and can see the Volvo parked, along with several other cars.

"Why hasn't he parked inside the base?" asks Chantal.

"Who knows, but it is our lucky day," I blip the car and we both climb in. The luxury of a modern all-electric Volvo contrasted with the utility of the jet fighter. I start the car and immediately we have sat nav and air conditioning as well as some softly playing classical music.

We settle down and then laugh.

"What else can you remember from this time?" asks Chantal.

"I know, it is so difficult to be in the detail of an actual historical event"

"We have been sent back to a time before the original time of Scrive and Chantal. I can remember we had high speed transit and the Klima Wars had finished. We were all living with tropus health management but I don't think it is even a thing yet."

"I'd guess we are at least 30 years earlier than Scrive and Chantal's original existence?" says Chantal.

"I'd say even further back. I think we have been sent to a time which avoids a paradox. You know to stop us from running into ourselves."

We both nod and try to work it out.

We have moved from being Watchers Farallon and Limantour in Bodø, Norway to being Wakeners after our intervention to protect Earth. Then, becoming Scrive and Chantal, propelled to a future time in late 21ˢᵗ Century beyond the Klima Wars. Both of us were separately zapped by Trigax Guns but somehow propelled back in time to 2022, when we find ourselves amid a historical event.

The event which started the Klima Wars.

Pockets

I start the drive to Central Kraków. It is only 15 kilometres away, according to the satnav.

"Pockets," says Chantal, "This outfit has pockets."

She produces her cellphone which is a broken-screened iPhone.

"The battery life is still good," she says, "And it's lucky I bought a charger yesterday in downtown Kyiv. They look different from how I remember. And this phone says it has 2 weeks of charge on it."

I'm struggling to remember the situation we left in Kyiv and know that the internet will only be as good as today's date, which is a few days before things really kicked off. But I also remember that a long-term state of war already existed in Ukraine, with the Russians attempting to encroach onto a sovereign state, even before the current conflict.

I remember that the Russians had snuck into Ukraine and Crimea not bearing their Russian identities. They were trying to clandestinely prise loose parts of the Ukrainian state to begin to consolidate the expansion of Russia.

Chantal begins to read from her phone, "Here, this article is dated 2021, but sets the scene:"

"The Russo-Ukrainian War is an ongoing war primarily involving Russia, pro-Russian forces, and Belarus on one side, and Ukraine and its international supporters on the other.

She continues, "Conflict began in February 2014 following the Revolution of Dignity and focused on the status of Crimea and parts of the Donbas, internationally recognised as part of Ukraine.

"The conflict includes the Russian annexation of Crimea (2014), the war in Donbas (2014–present), naval incidents, cyberwarfare, and political tensions.

Then she reads the part that I can remember, "Intentionally concealing its involvement, Russia gave military backing to separatists in the Donbas from 2014 onwards. Following the Euromaidan protests and a revolution resulting in the removal of pro-Russian President Viktor Yanukovych on 22 February 2014, pro-Russian unrest erupted in parts of Ukraine. Russian soldiers without insignia took control of strategic positions and infrastructure in the Ukrainian territory of Crimea."

I speak, "But this is frightening, using unmarked militia on a large scale to foment what amounts to a civil war, in Russia's interests."

"Yes," Chantal continues, "Unmarked Russian troops seized the Crimean Parliament and Russia organised a widely-criticised referendum, the outcome of which was for Crimea to join Russia."

She adds, "Russia then annexed Crimea. In April 2014, demonstrations by pro-Russian groups in the Donbas region of Ukraine escalated into a war between the Ukrainian military and Russian-backed separatists of the self-declared Donetsk and Luhansk republics."

I interrupt, "So Putin is all over this? He was trying to stretch the Russian borders to achieve his goal of becoming a mini-tsar, surrounded by fawning cronies."

I can't really concentrate on what Chantal is saying now. I'm using my Scrive-brain to negotiate heavy traffic on the way to the train station. We owe it to the Brits to find a clear parking space at Kraków Główny. I follow the signs to Galeria Krakowska, a large urban shopping mall adjacent to the station, and realise that the old stately-looking train station has been decommissioned and that here is now a huge new one built underground and connected to the shopping mall.

Then, miraculously, we are by an entrance to the mall and the station, and right next to it is a small row of unrestricted parking bays. I park the car tidily and we both climb out, carrying nothing but identification, phones, credit cards and the holdall.

"Shopping!" says Chantal gleefully, "We can go shopping!"

Koryciński cheese

We enter the mall, which is dizzily spread over multiple floors of galleried space, more like a cruise liner in concept.

I'm impressed that Chantal has an almost genetic affinity for the place and can lead us in a matter of moments to a quiet area away from the bustle of the busy retail area.

We are sitting in a coffee bar, and Chantal has ordered a couple of cortado coffees and baguettes with a koryciński cheese. I look at the faux wood panelling and authentic 'old-town' style writing, but then above it all I glimpse another sign - Green Caffe Nero.

"You'll notice that everything has cucumber or pickle with it, " says Chantal, "It's to get you in the mood for more shopping. Here let me finish what I was reading in the car."

She continues, "In August 2014, unmarked Russian military vehicles crossed the border into the Donetsk Republic. An undeclared war began between Ukrainian forces and separatists intermingled with Russian troops, although Russia denied the presence of its troops in the

Donbas. The war settled into a stalemate, with repeated failed attempts at ceasefire. In 2015, a package of agreements called Minsk II were signed by Russia and Ukraine, but a number of disputes prevented them from being fully implemented."

"That's Putin all over," I say, then, remembering I'm in a public space, I lower my voice to add, "Creating the illegal wedges for his next takeover attempt. Maybe he is trying to build a new iron curtain?"

Chantal whispers, "By 2019, 7% of Ukraine's territory was classified by the Ukrainian government as temporarily occupied territories, while the Russian government had indirectly acknowledged the presence of its troops in Ukraine. Then, from 2021, there was a major Russian military build-up around Ukraine's borders. NATO accused Russia of planning an invasion, which it denied."

She adds, "Russian President Vladimir Putin criticised the enlargement of NATO as a threat to his country and demanded Ukraine be barred from ever joining the military alliance. He also expressed Russian irredentist views, questioning Ukraine's right to exist, and stated Ukraine was wrongfully created by Soviet Russia."

"Irredentism?" I ask, "That's when a political movement claims and seeks to occupy territory they consider lost to their nation, isn't it?"

I add, "I think Russia goes on to recognise the two self-proclaimed separatist states in the Donbas and sends troops to both territories. Then Putin will announce a 'special military operation', which is widely condemned. We are right in the middle of this."

"Well, we still need shopping," says Chantal, "Let's think for a minute,"

She proceeds to make a list, to which I add big Swiss Army knife, torch, and backpacks x 2.

Then, she picks up a brochure showing the mall layout and speedily picks out a route around several stores to obtain our goods. I don't even know where she found the map.

"No-one is looking for us, I suggest we go together, rather than split up," she suggests, "I can find most items quickly with my superior shopping skills."

I'm inclined to agree.

Roads to Moscow

They crossed over the border, the hour before dawn
Moving in lines through the day
Most of our planes were destroyed on the ground where they lay
Waiting for orders we held in the wood
Word from the front never came
By evening the sound of the gunfire was miles away

Winter brought with her the rains, oceans of mud filled the roads
Gluing the tracks of their tanks to the ground while the sky filled with snow
And all that I ever
Was able to see
The fire in the air glowing red
Silhouetting the snow on the breeze

You'll never know, you'll never know which way to turn, which way to look
you'll never see us
As we're stealing through the blackness of the night
You'll never know, you'll never hear us
And the evening sings in a voice of amber, the dawn is surely coming
The morning roads lead to Stalingrad, and the sky is softly humming

I'm coming home, I'm coming home, now you can taste it in the wind, the
war is over
And I listen to the clicking of the train-wheels as we roll across the border
And now they ask me of the time that I was caught behind their lines and
taken prisoner
"They only held me for a day, a lucky break, " I say they turn and listen closer

I'll never know, I'll never know why I was taken from the line and all the
others
To board a special train and journey deep into the heart of holy Russia
And it's cold and damp in the transit camp, and the air is still and sullen
And the pale sun of October whispers the snow will soon be coming
And I wonder when I'll be home again and the morning answers "Never"
And the evening sighs, and the steely Russian skies go on forever

Al Stewart

Across Poland

I wasn't sure what to expect from the Polish trains. It turned out that they had a very smart-looking bullet train that could get us to Warsaw, and from there it would be a simple, though lengthy, journey to Berlin.

With our newly acquired supplies, courtesy of shopping ninja Chantal, we were ready to board the blue and silver bullet train to Warsaw. Two hours and 19 minutes to cover the 300-kilometre distance. Compare that with the 500 kilometres in 6 hours from Warsaw to Berlin. The direct Kraków to Berlin route takes around ten hours, including a couple of bus stages, but our 'two sides of a triangle' route was better because we would be on just two trains for the whole journey.

Compared with our lives as Farallon and Limantour, our acquired Presences of Scrive and Chantal had to make do with lengthy travelling.

We boarded the train, an EIP Express InterCity Premium train, also called a Pendolino. For the 21st Century they were very comfortable with climate control and reclining seats.

That's about when Chantal asked, "Did you get that?"

"Get what?"

"It was a message, a message from Tomales. Somehow, she's in Russia. I think she said something about Krasnodar Krai. Remember, her name is Charlie now."

I strained to see if I could also receive anything from Tomales by way of a Watcher message. Nothing, but I remembered that Tomales and Limantour had been particularly close and so I was not surprised that their linkage was stronger than mine.

My special power as a Watcher was related to gravity, and Limantour's was as 'the Mistress of Chaos'. Tomales had power as a shapeshifter. More than simple transformations, she could use hypnogogic mind inducement to cast a sphere of belief around her chosen target.

I guessed that Tomales would be helping us to get into Russia but for reasons I couldn't comprehend. Maybe she had sold out to the dark forces.

Then, Scrive's impulses reminded me that he knew Charlie very well and that they had worked together often.

"I think there's a way to get to Charlie that is easier than Watcher back-channels!"

"What's that?"

"Mobile phone, she kept the same number for years - so long as it works in the past!"

I looked up Charlie on Scrive's phone. Sure enough, it was there, along with a string of addresses and even an old-fashioned land-line number.

I hit dial, to see what would happen. There was a short pause and then I could hear the number ringing.

"Hey, Scrive!"

"Hey, Charlie! How are you doing?"

"Yes, it's been a long time and now we find ourselves in the past, moving forward at human pace! How weird is that? Say, how did you find me - I was just signalling to Limantour!"

"I know, I'm with Limantour. We are in Poland. It's a long story."

"It can't be as long as mine! I'm in the middle of Russia just when Putin decides to throw a hissy fit."

"Hissy fit! I think it's a bit more than that."

"I agree, and some of his best buddies are not best pleased, either. Say, did you get Trigaxed? I was about to get onto the subway in New York when I was hit with a Trigax. It blasted me to near Saint Petersburg, and when I woke up everyone was speaking Russian. My Persona Charlie was ever resourceful and the next thing I know I'm being recruited by the Tambov Bratva to run security for the Ozero Dacha Community. You could say I'm collecting Vladimirs!"

I didn't understand the last remark, but Charlie went on to say, "Yeah, that's Vladimir Smirnov - one of the businessman owners of the Ozero Community, Vladimir

Barsukov - the alleged boss of the Tambov gang and Vladimir Putin!"

Tomales was always a great shapeshifter so it didn't really surprise me that she had managed to get into a new security role at one of Putin's places.

Charlie adds, "When Vladimir Putin returned from his KGB posting in Dresden in early 1990, it was prior to the formal establishment of the Ozero cooperative. You might remember how he set fire to all the records of everything in Dresden, so that he would have a clean start in Saint Petersburg?"

"Yes, " I answer, "I remember that young Putin learned his gangster moves in Dresden and put them into effect when he set up shop in Saint Petersburg."

Charlie adds, "All he needed were some tie-ins with ruthless gangsters like the Tambov Bratva and he could set about running the port of Saint Petersburg and trafficking whatever he wanted through it. Any sign of resistance and he'd use the muscle from the local gangsters as enforcement."

I knew I'd read about this somewhere before, but it was interesting to have Charlie's direct account of the situation.

"Putin also acquired property on the banks of Lake Komsomolskoye. That's a short drive north-east from Saint Petersburg, and then later his Italianate palace - a proper villain's lair - near Gelendzhik, Krasnodar Krai, on the Black Sea. It's unmarked on maps but along the coast from Sail Rock about 7 kilometres by very twisty roads through what is marked as private green park land."

"Separately, he acquired land in the Ozero Community, which west of Moscow. Then he encouraged others to build close by. You could say they were his cronies, but later became some of the most powerful people in Russia. Others from his inner circle bought land around this area and built several villas close to each other to form a gated and guarded community.

"That's where I was first recruited. Word was out that they need someone to boost his security because Putin was about to do something big."

Charlie paused, and then continued, "I guess it is my own Watcher Intervention against Putin. I decided it would be easier to work from the inside. The worst that could happen would be that my presence as Charlie gets bounced along the timeline again."

I realised that Charlie was referring to what had happened to Scrive, Chantal and Charlie, each of whom had been blasted with a Trigax railgun but were then re-instated at an earlier point in history.

Charlie paused, but then continued, "Putin has become hung up on poison attempts after all the ones he ordered. Hence the large space around him on most appearances. You know the kind of thing? The laughably long tables. It's not all about his -ahem- ego."

Chantal spoke, "You remember? He tried poison on his main political opposition Alexander Navalny in Moscow and attempted to silence the Skripals, in Salisbury, England with poison from a scent bottle dispatched by two hapless killers."

I was grateful that as Watchers we all had encyclopaedic

powers of historical recall. I remembered too, that Putin contracted for the killing of Anna Politkovskaya, who wrote the heavily critical reference book 'Putin's Russia'. She was shot four times in an elevator in her block of flats. She had already been poisoned prior to this, on a Russian plane, but was finally killed in this third attempt on Putin's birthday.

A week after her assassination, Alexander Litvinenko accused Putin of sanctioning the murder. Two weeks after this statement, Litvinenko was poisoned with Polonium also on the third attempt of two hitmen Lugovoi and Kovtun sent by Russia's FSB spy agency.

Litvinenko's poisoning was remarkably similar to the thallium poisoning of KGB defector Nikolai Khokhlov whom Anna Politkovskaya had interviewed for Novaya Gazeta. Politkovskaya also blew the lid off the horrendous fear driven conditions in the Russian Army.

Putin made it known that he would regard offshore assassinations as legitimate, which led to further killings. He also wanted to re-balance the books from the complex state selloffs which he had engineered. Sometimes the men in charge were paying him well enough, but other times he could place new younger men in position, who would follow his demands. It became an era when old Russian businessmen were pushed out of windows.

The former pro-government Chechen commander and FSB officer Movladi Baisarov was shot dead in Moscow. Allegedly, Baisarov intended to give evidence that proved his political opponents' guilt of kidnapping and murder and additionally to give testimony about Politkovskaya's assassination.

Journalist Vyacheslav Izmailov indicated that armed

men close to Ramzan Kadyrov had been sent to Moscow with orders to kill three people: Politkovskaya, Baisarov and Gantamirov.

Then a former KGB officer Oleg Gordievsky asserted that the murders of Zelimkhan Yandarbiev, Yuri Shchekochikhin, Anna Politkovskaya, Alexander Litvinenko, and others meant that FSB had returned to the old KGB practice of government-ordered political assassinations. It all led back to Putin.

Gordievsky himself was subsequently poisoned, allegedly by a Russian agent, but survived.

Charlie continues, "A bank account linked to this new-formed Ozero cooperative association was opened, allowing money to be deposited and used by all account holders in accordance with the Russian law on cooperatives.

"By 2012 members of the Ozero cooperative had assumed top positions in Russian government and business and became very successful financially.

"But this not where he has his palace, is it?" I asked.

"No, that's in a different part of Russia. He built the palace at Krasnodar Krai, on the Black Sea. It's Putin's overlord mansion. It was like he'd read the comedy Evil Overlord meme from the internet and then tried to implement everything it described, right down to the swimming pool which can be used as a bunker. Think Thunderbird's Tracey Island crossed with Versailles, in Extra Large. Doors - much higher than needed, Tables much longer than needed. You get the picture."

Charlie paused, and I realised why Scrive liked her so

much.

"So, should we join you? We are on our way to Berlin, via Warsaw..."

"It'd be foolhardy, wouldn't it?"

"Has that ever stopped us?"

I looked over to Chantal, who was nodding her assent to make the trip to join Charlie. Things were just kicking off.

Международный аэропорт Шереметьево имени А. С. Пушкина

Chantal was already onto the system to find out how to get from Warsaw Central to the airport. It turned out to be a 20-minute ride on the metro. We'd need to look out for the signs at Warsaw Centrum station. This early 21st century land-based travel was so much more complicated and slower than our Watcher methods of getting around.

"But how will we get through Moscow to meet with Charlie?" I ask.

"Remember Tomales had that special power?" says Chantal, "It was so annoying. Whenever we wanted to go out anywhere, she could transform into the best outfits, instantly. Shapeshifting and mind warp. I guess that Charlie is the same."

With that, a text arrives on my cellphone. It was from Charlie, addressed to Scrive.

"Scrive. I'll meet you both at the airport. Stick with me and you'll get into anywhere. C x x x"

I hold up the phone for Chantal to see.

"Charlie's going to bust us into Putin's place using one of her psychic mind warps," says Chantal, "I can feel the chaos level rising."

With airport delays, we arrive in Moscow around three hours later. We land at Международный аэропорт Шереметьево имени А. С. Пушкина and I realise that my Russian is as good as every other language and I could instantly see Sheremetyevo Alexander S. Pushkin International Airport and even say *Mezhdunarodnyy aeroport Sheremetyevo imeni A. S. Pushkina*.

They say the name was given after a competition and the Russian poet's name of Alexander Pushkin won.

I wasn't sure how we'd find Charlie, but I assumed she would know her way around and be able to get to our terminal in the busiest airport in Russia.

The architecture reminds me of a 1960's dream of a modernist styled airbase. It is all extruded sweeping concrete lines and with a strangely stylish flying saucer shaped terminal B.

Unsurprisingly, Sheremetyevo International Airport became a state-owned enterprise amidst the dissolution of the Soviet Union but didn't take long to be turned into a joint stock company, ready to be plucked by affluent Russian businessmen.

"We just need to wait here and Charlie will show up," says Chantal. She points to a nearby cafe - Pelmeni.

"Let's sit here," she says.

We both order Russian Street food - chebureki with a lamb filling. They arrive and are like flattened empanada, made with a soft shell of dough and seasoned with onions and black pepper. It is a good way to change gear into thinking like Russia. The 'coffee' which we order arrives and they are Raf - a white frothy vanilla coffee. We must have passed the Russian test or we'd have been given Cappuccino or Americano.

"I see you are getting into it!" says a voice. It is Charlie striding toward us like a Russian fashion icon.

"Oooh!" says Chantal, "I love the outfit!"

Charlie is wearing a striking feminine top of striped dark blue, brown, and white. It looks almost like she is wearing a sash and below she has similarly coloured mini-skirt and black tights.

"It's a Miroslava Duma colour block," explains Charlie, "You want me to fix you up with something like this?"

"All in good time," says Chantal, "But I will hold you to it."

They both laugh and I notice we are starting to attract attention.

"Okay, I'll have to get you into my office," says Charlie.

"It's at the Ozero - where I've just come from, actually."

She flips open a slim black briefcase.

"Here," she says, as she hands over two small white cards, like hotel keys.

Пропуск безопасности -Propusk bezopasnosti Security Passes.

I can tell that they are electronic, like the kind that they use on some Metro systems. Then she digs into her bag again and produces two full passport sized Visas.

"It's okay, " she says, "You can literally peel the back off and then stick these into your passports. They are self-adhesive - just find a blank passport page. No-one here will argue when they see them. They are Russian Service Visas, which is one step down from a full head of state Diplomatic Visa.

She pulls a couple of small photos from an envelope, "You'll need these too. A photo which you can staple into the front of your passports. These two pictures are up-to-date enough and I've already fed them into the Russian Border Control system."

"We didn't seem to have any trouble getting into Russia," says Chantal.

"I also changed your APCS profiles at SVO," answers Charlie, dropping into jargon. The Russian Federal Security Service (FSB) are using an automated passport control system at Sheremetyevo. It relies on biometric data and foreign passport recognition to allow Russian passengers to move through border control with fewer movement restrictions. I fed both Scrive Mallinson and Chantal le Strang's profiles into the system, although I was surprised to see you are both travelling on Dutch passports?"

"We just wanted something that could get us around most of Europe with no hassle," I explain, "It's so much more hassle compared with being a Watcher."

Charlie and the dead dog

"So, Charlie, tell us what you are doing here?" asks Chantal.

"I've had to learn about this particular piece of history since I've been in Russia running security," says Charlie, "After I was Trigaxed in New York, I awoke to find found myself in Saint Petersburg."

"But you haven't told us what you are doing?" I ask Charlie. I know she is hot on security matters and assume it is something in that area.

"I've had to resurrect some of my old skills," she answers, "Ozero Dacha Community wanted someone who is the best at security and containment. Someone who can identify leaks before they happen and has the skills to be able to run disinformation strategies.

She listed some examples, "The Kremlin has everything: click farms, ransomware, code injectors, cross-site scripting attacks, data breach catalogues, malware and virus infection, distributed denial of service, credential stuffing, brute force attacks, weak password and authentication hacking, social engineering, spam and phishing, insider threats and sensitive data leak tracking."

"Whoa, Charlie, this isn't an interview!" says Chantal.

All three of us laugh. The waiter reappears and asks us if we'd like something else. I order a beer and the others both order black coffees.

"Well, as Scrive knows, I'm pretty hot on all of those techniques and so the word soon got around the Ozero about my abilities. They asked me to help them in more ways and I was prepared to oblige when it was non-life-threatening to others. Not only that, but they also wanted me to help with some off-property matters too."

Charlie adds, "The Ozero community houses a whole group of Putin followers in their summer retreats. It is as if the inner circle of Putin has all got places together and can meet around one another's' extensive pools. Think of the New York elite going to the Hamptons and then add some extra bling."

She continues, "There's the Fursenkos, Andrei and Sergey, they handle or have handled the Center for Strategic Research Northwest, the Ministry of Education and Science of the Russian Federation (2004-2012), Andrei is Assistant to the President of the Russian Federation (2012-present)."

"I see, the whole Russian Federation, between Putin and this man?" asks Chantal, "And Education, as well!"

Charlie continues, "Then Sergey Fursenko runs the Lentransgaz subsidiary of Gazprom, and president of National Media Group, as well as president of the Russian Football Union (2010-2012).

"Gazprom, the massive sold-off state gas producing firm, which sells much of its output to the west," says Chantal.

Charlie nods, "Yury Kovalchuk, on the board of Bank Rossiya and a co-owner of National Media Group. Add in Viktor Myachin the former Director-General of Bank Rossiya, CEO of the investment company "Abros", a subsidiary of Rossiya Bank (2004-present): This investment company owns 51% of the Соraз, a big insurance company in Russia."

"It's quite a list, the Federation, Education, Energy Production, Banking and Investment," says Chantal.

Charlie smiles, "Nikolay Shamalov who is a Board member for Vyborg Shipyard, Bank Rossiya, Gazprombank, as well as Vladimir Smirnov who is on the board of Techsnabexport. Oh yes, and Vladimir Yakunin the deputy minister of transport as well as president of Russian Railways."

"Oh, I see, just add shipping, news dissemination, more banking, and export business," says Chantal, "It's like one of those board games where you have to buy up the industries."

Charlie grimaces, "It' not just in Russia either. For example, in the U.K. it is unsettling that the much-disgraced Prime Minister has risen through Mayor of London and then foreign secretary yet casts a wake of bad tales about himself.

She adds, "Like in other countries, the UK Conservative party gains much of its funds from the Russians. Usually oligarchs and kleptocrats.

"I think the biggest single donor to help keep the Tories in office is the financier Ms. Lubov Chernukhin, who has donated £700,000. She became a British nationalsome ten years ago and is married to Vladimir Chernukhin, a former deputy finance minister under Putin."

She holds up her phone, "Look, here is Ms Chernukhin with Liz Truss, the then international trade secretary, at a 'ladies' night', recorded on Instagram."

Charlie adds, "This British so-called leader thought it appropriate to take hospitality on multiple occasions from a Russian-born media mogul, Evgeny Lebedev, whose oligarch father Alexander had a strong relationship with President Putin and the Kremlin."

" 'Beggars belief' springs to mind," says Chantal clutching her phone, "Look, I've found this newspaper article which claims the former foreign secretary had been branded a security risk by a senior cabinet minister."

Chantal continues, "In a front-page story the same Sunday paper quotes the cabinet minister in conversation with another unnamed cabinet minister: 'There will be things in his private life that we don't know about ... there's the danger that people leak what they have over him or blackmail him with it.' "

I recollect that this man was often placed at the centre of controversies during his time in office. He nurtured buffoonery to hide his own deeply flawed professionalism and was a serial rule breaker with a strong reputation for lies. It didn't end well for him.

Charlie begins, "One start point is when the U.K. foreign secretary made a trip to Italy for a party. It ended when that man - who later became the U.K. Prime Minister -

was seen at an airport looking as if he had slept in his clothes, struggling to walk in a straight line and telling other passengers he had had a heavy night."

"My kind of party," said Chantal, "Well maybe not the sleeping in clothes part. Come to think of it not the 'can't walk in a straight line' part either."

Charlie continues, "It's common knowledge and has been reported that he was at a party thrown by billionaire socialite and media owner Evgeny Lebedev, who is known for hosting uproarious parties for the rich and famous at his converted castle near Perugia."

"But wait a minute," I ask Charlie, "Didn't that same Prime Minister ignore advice from MI5 and MI6 and award a peerage to Lebedev? Lord Evgeny Lebedev, son of Alexander Lebedev, himself a former KGB officer who gave the Prime Minister lots of money?"

"Just don't say those kinds of things out loud around here," answers Charlie, "Although it is borne out by his entry of ministerial interests on the Foreign Office website, where he declared he had an overnight stay with Lebedev travelling 'accompanied by a spouse, family member or friend'.

"I expect the press have pictures of his companion of the evening," said Chantal, "There seem to be a wide selection to choose from."

Charlie grins and then says, "Of course, like so many other things in his life, there were no explanations, for example, of where he had been, who he was with or the reason for the visit. And yet, at that time, he was under great scrutiny. The day before flying out he had been in Brussels for talks with the US secretary of state, Mike

Pompeo, and other NATO leaders to discuss how to deal with Russia in the aftermath of nerve agent poisonings in Salisbury."

"Lie, deny and move on!" says Chantal wryly.

Charlie adds, "In the U.K. Evgeny Lebedev sold significant shares in the Evening Standard and Independent website to an entity in the Cayman Islands with strong links to Saudi Arabia. It was speculated the sale warranted investigation, given the public requirement for accurate news and free expression of opinion."

"I see, " says Chantel, "So we have possible Russian influence in British politics too!"

Charlie adds, "Evgeny Lebedev was educated in the UK and is on record as saying he is 'proud to be a British citizen and considers Britain my home'. He acknowledged his father 'was a foreign intelligence agent of the KGB but explains that he is not some agent of Russia'. He said his father spent his time campaigning against corruption and illegal financial dealings and his family 'has a record of standing up for press freedom' in Russia."

She adds, "Lebedev is on record for writing a letter to Putin, in which he urged the Russian president:

'As a Russian citizen I plead with you to stop Russians killing their Ukrainian brothers and sisters. As a British citizen I ask you to save Europe from war. As a Russian patriot I plead that you prevent any more young Russian soldiers from dying needlessly. As a citizen of the world, I ask you to save the world from annihilation.'

Charlie continues, "But then, to top everything, there's the strange case of the dead dog. Evgeny Lebedev's dog, yet another Vladimir, a large white Borzoi, like a Russian wolfhound, was found dead on his Umbrian estate."

"Did he call it Vladimir after the President?" asked Chantal, "Only that would be asking for trouble."

Charlie looks around the cafe, "The dog was said to be Lebedev's pride and joy. His Instagram account was full of pictures of the huge dog, which was clearly an important part of his life. Lebedev has told associates that he believes the dog was poisoned and that the poisoning was a strong message from Moscow."

I noticed that Charlie emphasised poisoned and wondered if there was more.

Kleptocrat

I thought about what Charlie described.

It sums up the thuggish kleptocracy that Putin engineered, progressively ever since his time in Dresden. He was a bit player there, but learned fast, when he burned all the evidence of his wrongdoing and corruption.

Then he moved to become aide to St Petersburg mayor Anatoly Sobchak, whom he had soon displaced - himself becoming deputy mayor. With the help of the local crime lords, he became the main man, wiping out anyone that dared to oppose him. Onward to Moscow as head of the FSB spy agency in the Kremlin and then to put his arms around the entire Motherland.

Charlie begins, "Don't worry - This is my private Intervention. I've not swallowed Putin's doctrine, but I can see it leads to a bad place. However, it is best to look as if you are believers when you are so close to his power base. Let me summarise:"

She continues, "In Vladimir Putin's Russia, opaque financial flows and a murky network of ex-KGB officers come together in a distinctive system of corruption."

She pauses to orders pancakes from a waiter. I notice she asks for blintz rather than blini. It should arrive with cream cheese.

But it is what she describes about Putin that is what I remember. My sense of history is still challenged by what was happening around me, but I was so much closer to real events now, being Farallon in Scrive's body.

Charlie continues, "Putin's approach serves dual purposes: Those at the top follow the imperative of self-enrichment, but they also find corruption a highly effective tool for consolidating domestic political control and projecting power abroad.

"In Russia, omnipresent corruption makes property claims and business ventures contingent on the whims of the authorities, while keeping officials themselves permanently under the threat of selective punishment.

"Abroad, corruption serves as a key lever of Russian influence in other post-Soviet states, as well as a tool for undermining established democracies. An Orwellian control of the state media assists keep the citizens unaware of Putin's duplicity. The combination of misinformation and news suppression creates a complete alternative reality."

Her blintz arrives as she looks at us both: "Yet Putin knows it also creates vulnerabilities making Russia prone to reckless and extreme measures. Although Russia's kleptocracy is a self-sustaining system, it faces a growing backlash in the form of international sanctions and domestic discontent. He's sold the state to his cronies at knock-down prices, but at some point, the rest of Russia will start to notice."

Chantal asks, "But hasn't the restoration of Russia's status as a world power has been a top ideological priority of the country's Putin-era government"

Charlie nods, but adds, "The Russian economy poses a significant impediment to this goal. Even during the relative boom years, the size of the country's economy never matched its geopolitical ambitions. For example, compare the vastness of Russia with the economic success of China."

Charlie tastes the blintz and smiles, "Delicious. But let's think...A combination of low oil prices and Western economic sanctions imposed in response to Russia's aggression in Ukraine hobbled Russia's ability to project power via economic means. The Ukrainian conflict goes back over many years. It was occurring well before the 2022 conflict started."

My composite of Scrive and Farallon was thinking that the Russian regime uses economic resources as a tool the benefit of Russia's narrow elite. It uses large-scale corruption internationally both to undermine democratic resolve and principles in established democracies, and to influence foreign political and economic elites.

This process is enabled by the extreme concentration of wealth in the hands of a powerful elite, and the extraordinary amount of that wealth that is held outside of the country.

At the same time, the super-rich responsible for this capital flight from Russia do not fully control this wealth themselves. Russia's property rights and the rule of law is such that these oligarchs' wealth building is entirely contingent on their standing with the Putin regime.

All through Putin's tenure, formerly powerful oligarchs who show political disloyalty or simply lose internal power struggles have been arrested on politically motivated charges and had their assets seized by the state for distribution to other oligarchs in better political standing. Sometimes people are pushed out of windows.

As a result, it is well understood by Russia's oligarch class that it is in their personal interest to use their wealth in ways to maintain the regime's political favour.

In some cases, this means domestic spending on important political constituencies (such as raising wages or subsidising social benefits prior to elections), or contributions to political projects such as the infrastructure for the Olympics or other sporting events. Massive events which can also be used as money laundries.

Perhaps more significant are the instances when this same phenomenon appears abroad; such cases reveal the nature of Russian kleptocracy's interaction with the world of international politics.

Charlie continues, "It is not unusual for wealthy citizens of any country to engage in personal international initiatives—philanthropic, political, or otherwise—that serve as instruments of their countries' soft power. What is unusual in the Russian case is the motivation of buying political goodwill as insurance against expropriation. It creates a consequent close alignment of wealthy Russians' international activities with the Russian state and its foreign policy goals."

She looks at the remains of coffee, "These kinds of

international activities fall along a spectrum. At the more innocuous end are projects like the Dialogue of Civilizations Research Institute (DOC), a Berlin think tank with a Russia-sympathetic world outlook founded in 2016 by Vladimir Yakunin, a billionaire and former head of Russia's state railways, who maintains a close relationship with Vladimir Putin and is rumoured to have a KGB past."

Chantel asks, "So did his cronies help fund his war efforts? He must need a huge amount of money to run wars like the Ukrainian conflict?"

Charlie signals for a refill of coffee, "At the more dramatic end, the oligarch Konstantin Malofeev, a billionaire investment banker, is reported to be involved in helping to finance and organize separatists fighting in eastern Ukraine. Putin himself arranged for the split of Sberbank, which gave him a golden share after putting 50% of the citizen money into a state-owned repository. Think about it. It's quite a war chest."

Charlie shakes her head, "And let's not forget how far this net spreads. There's significant influence in London, among politicians and in New York, for example."

She turns her refill cup of plain, black, coffee around, "The ability to purchase entry into these communities gives wealthy Russians access to the social circles of Western political and economic elites, as do purchases of high-profile assets like professional sports teams and generous donations to universities and cultural institutions. We've all heard Britain described as the 'Butler to the World'."

"Putin started it with the people he put around himself in Saint Petersburg and then the people he moved to continue to support him in Moscow. No wonder he built the Ozero to provide a network for his closest allies."

In between these extremes, however, lies a wide range of influence activities that are more difficult to identify or to quantify, but which nevertheless are important in advancing the Russian elite's interests and objectives.

For example, the trend of wealthy Russians buying high-end luxury real estate in select urban markets (London, Manhattan, Miami, and so on) has a practical component—transferring wealth to jurisdictions with more solid rule of law, in a sector whose practice make it easier to conceal funds' origins—but also a political one. The ability to purchase entry into these communities gives wealthy Russians access to the social circles of Western political and economic elites, as do purchases of high-profile assets like professional sports teams and generous donations to universities and cultural institutions.

On their own, of course, these purchases and donations do not distinguish Russian oligarchs from any other members of the global elite. These activities must also be viewed through the lens of the politicised nature of wealth in today's Russia described above.

When a museum accepts a donation from a Russian businessman, or a sports league allows a wealthy Russian to purchase one of its franchises, it is de facto legitimising the kleptocratic system through which that wealth was accumulated. These transactions in a subtler way serve to normalise the large-scale corruption that allows a select few Russians to become tremendously wealthy, and by extension, normalises the Russian regime itself.

"So how do we get to yours, then?" asks Chantal to Charlie.

"It's easier than you might think, she explains, "I have a chauffeur."

"What? Is it in Moscow?"

"No, it is in Moscow Oblast, but around 46 kilometres from the centre," replied Charlie, "Oh and when I say chauffeur, I should really say pilot. One from the military. We'll be flying in a helicopter to Ozero. Although I have a military pilot, we'll be using the commercial version of the chopper, so it will be a short comfortable ride. Shall we make our way?"

I looked at Chantal, and she looked at me. We were in this now and needed to follow it through. It was like Charlie/Tomales was staging another Watcher Intervention, but for reasons that we didn't understand.

KA-62

Charlie leads us to quieter part of the airport and onward to Terminal A. I can see several monied-looking Russians standing around chatting. It's all shiny marble floors, plate glass and tasteful honey-coloured wood. It looks as if it has all been recently refurbished.

"The money buys 'hush' around here," explains Charlie, "In more senses than one."

A regulation-looking pilot strides towards Charlie and greets her.

"This is Antanov," she explains, introducing each of us to him.

He smiles back, "Great, let's move straight through to the 'plane," he says, "It's a Kamov Ka-62, which is the civilian version of a Russian fighter helicopter. I find it easier to travel without the armaments unless absolutely necessary."

We walk outside of the terminal and on to the apron, where a few helicopters have been parked. He takes us to a shiny red one, with black picked out around the windows. It looks quite luxurious from outside.

"Look, over there," he says, pointing to a drab military helicopter in green camouflage colours. It has a prominent red star and seems to have less windows than ours.

"That's a Ka-60 - the military version of our helicopter. Designed for menace rather than comfort."

Inside, the helicopter reminds me of something that would be designed by a teenage computer-gamer. It has what looks like black and grey rally-cross seats with red seatbelts that would not look out of place on an ejector seat.

"I'm told that it is the glamorous hosts that sell these helicopters, at special air shows," explained Antanov, "They are a snip at $9 million."

As we climb in, I can see the huge flat panel displays which have replaced all the conventional dials, and two reassuringly vintage looking leather pilot's chairs.

"How come you don't get the snazzy seats?" I ask Antanov.

He smiles as he explains, "I'm a real pilot. I don't need all of the gimmicks when I can have comfort."

Then, someone else climbs into the copter. Slender, athletic and with her blonde hair cut into a blunt bob, she smiles as she approaches us.

"Oh, I should introduce you all. This is Christina, Christina Nott. She is another security agent and one I have known for a long time," says Antanov, "She'll be acting as our co-pilot this afternoon."

I notice that see is wearing a bright emerald green jacket and matching trousers, when Chantal pipes up, "Ooh, I love the Gucci!"

Christina smiles casually and say, "Why thank you, and I love your zebra print. Our greens complement one another!"

I see the brief flicker of pleasure that crosses Chantal's face and can sense a massive shopping spree in the near future.

Christina and Antanov take their places in the pilot seats and prepare for a take-off. "Flight time will be around ten minutes," announces Antanov, "And you might want to wear the headphones."

With that, he starts the engines which are surprisingly quiet, at least whilst we are still on the ground. Then, suddenly, the ground is far below us and we are manoeuvring for the flight to Charlie's new base camp, in the Ozero Community, to the west of a cloudy Moscow.

Despite the comparative quiet, I save my questions until we arrive at Ozero.

Ozero

Ozero from the air doesn't seem all that special. I can only see a river, cottages, the outskirts of forests and a small river running through the area.

Christina, on the headphones points out the village of Leshkovo in the Istrinsky district of Moscow Region.

She points to several perimeter fences and explains that it is here where splendid, opulent palaces of the common people stand.

She talks about one, as an example, a lot belonging to a 'simple miner' and Secretary of the General Council of the 'United Russia Party', Sergey Neverov.

Christina explains, "Neverov loves to portray himself as a blue-collar worker. He was never involved in business, and over the last few years was living on the taxpayers' dime in the civil service. He doesn't have a lot of income but somehow managed to acquire 'a cottage lot' worth 92 million roubles which he registered under his mother-in-law's name – a 75-year-old pensioner from Novokuznetsk.

"Neverov explains that he acquired it and will build all of it up on 'money gained from the sale of a 67 square metre two-bedroom apartment in Novokuznetsk'.

"Would a 67 square metre apartment in Novokuznetsk provision an enormous lot on the bank of the Moscow river and a home which, in all likelihood, is twice as big as the Central Pioneer Palace in Novokuznetsk?

"Instead, we deduce that Neverov is an abominable liar and bribe taker, just like everyone else in 'United Russia'. And his secret sources of income can be explained in just one word: 'corruption'."

We climb out of the helicopter and I notice we are on a building site.

Charlie explains, "This plot of land is not finished yet. When it is, another oligarch will be invited to bid for it. It gives us somewhere to be based for this operation. And don't worry, I have been given permission to use this until the plot is ready for handover. The main block is complete, although there is still much work to be completed on the connecting buildings and in some of the underground areas."

We walk toward the main building, which, to my eyes looks finished. When we are all in the building, I can see that just the front reception area has been completed, but that most of the building is ready for an interior designer's touch. The completed lobby interior reminds me of the airport terminal where we had picked up the helicopter and I deduce that this must be the latest fashion in Moscow.

There are several seating areas, a table, and a small catering area, with a microwave and a coffee maker stood on the worktop.

The rest of the building looks unfinished, with plasterboard and electric fitments visible.

We all sit around a large, flat airport lounge styled coffee table.

"Time for some explanations," says Charlie.

Paradise or scramjets?

We sit together around a low table in the lobby of this newly constructed Oligarch paradise. I guess the furnishings are all temporary, brought in by a design firm to create some ambiance for prospective purchasers.

Charlie begins, "I was contacted in Saint Petersburg by Christina. She asked me to meet her in a fancy restaurant. Said it was important."

Christina adds, "Yes, I arranged to meet at Gogol, which is a lovely Russian restaurant situated just off Nevsky Prospect."

I saw Antanov nod in appreciation of the choice. He walked to the coffee machine and was fiddling with it.

Charlie adds, "Gogol was so traditional and you had to ring a little bell to call the waitress! A first for me!"

Christina takes over the conversation, "Well, I didn't know anything about you, but my contact in Moscow had said you would be useful for this mission. My contact has a codename 'Blackbird' and Antanov and myself are both run by him."

"What, so you are both agents?" asks Chantal.

"Yes, we both have links to the FSB, which is like the renewal of the KGB," answers Antanov, "Although Christina bought her way out, some time ago."

Antanov carries a tray of five small coffee cups across to the coffee table, "Blackbird explained that Charlie had been sent to Russia and was an important asset, specialising in security. She was to be asked to assist us to penetrate Putin's Kremlin. Putin is up to no good and will need to be disabled."

I ask, "But what about Blackbird? And both of you, come to that. Won't you be seen as traitors to Russia if you start to mess with internal politics?"

Christina sips the coffee, "That's why we asked Charlie to intervene. She was talent scouted by one of Blackbird's agents. And by the same token, you both as well; Scrive and Chantal. All three of you have no trail. There's no record of you in any of our systems, yet you all seem to possess significant skills. You are all clean."

Charlie speaks, "Well when I got here, I decided that I would stage an Intervention. Scrive and Chantal know what I mean."

"Intervention?" asks Christina, "Are you all addicts or something?"

"No, it is hard to explain," says Chantal. I notice what I take to be an overhead light flickering a couple of times then she says, "We are all Watchers. Not from this place, but of this place."

"Sounds kind of unusual," says Christina, looking at us all carefully, "Although I noticed that there is something kind of glitchy about your appearances. You sometimes seem to flicker, as if you are not really here. And you need to tell us, where have you come from?"

Charlie continues, "Well observed. You won't believe our story, about how we were tracking the future and then each of us got zapped with a railgun which brought us back to this place. It cannot be co-incidence. It must be for a reason."

Christina looks puzzled, "But rail guns don't exist as 'zapping' devices. There's only a few in existence around the world, and they are used to fire other projectiles."

"They become mainstream in the mid 21st Century," says Chantal, "After the success of the MARAUDER Project - That's Magnetically Accelerated Ring to Achieve Ultra-high Directed Energy and Radiation - which is a US program and probably still classified. It's the Chinese that perfect the plasma technology, initially for use at sea on the Haiyangshan, but then into space. A 'bracelet of charms', it will be called and it will be used to police newly-defined off-grid areas of the planet Earth."

"We can check with Blackbird about the Marauder project," says Christina.

"Check also on Tsircon, then," says Charlie, "Its a a scramjet powered manoeuvring anti-ship hypersonic cruise missile, designated 3M22, currently in production by Russia. It is still a state secret though."

Christina nods, "I worked and lived in the Arkhangelsk region of Russia, near the White Sea. Nearby, in Nenoksa, was the test range for cruise and sea-based ballistic missiles. I can remember a failed launch of a scramjet sample; It was called the 3M22.

"I recollect there was land testing before it was to be placed on a sea-going platform, the fifth-generation Haski nuclear submarine designed by Malakhit naval machine-building bureau in St. Petersburg."

Chantel grimaced, "You wait until the Chinese do a deal with the Russians and plasma railguns take to the skies. We can't stop all of it, but we can deflect some of it, with Charlie's Intervention."

Christina looks at us again, "You'll need to convince us. Despite being recommended by Blackbird, you could still be Kremlin plants, sent to infiltrate whatever Blackbird is trying to achieve."

I suddenly remembered Chantal when I'd first seen her back in the hotel. I remembered the burn marks on her skin. Now wasn't the most obvious time to rip off my shirt, but I did so anyway, to the astonishment of everyone else.

"Here," I said, "I've got a Trigax burn; three streams of plasma which were fired directly at me from an orbiting railgun. It was around 40 years into the future and I was projected back to now. I suggest that maybe Christina does a quick check of Limantour, sorry Chantal, and Charlie. I know Chantal has the burns and I expect Charlie does too.

Charlie nods. Chantal says, "I'm not going to destroy my lovely green zebra suit though."

Then there's an awkward moment, which culminates in Christina marching Chantal and Charlie to the nearby restroom.

"That's some powerful weapon," says Antanov to me. He pauses and then adds, "You seem to be genuine to me, Scrive, or whatever your name is."

We both laugh at the improbability of the situation and I can see that Antanov is trying to process the information.

"So, this could still be part of an elaborate back-story? A complex 'legend' made up to convince us that you are who you say you are."

I decide to tell Antanov more of our story. That we three, plus another one, are entities from outside of his universe. That we've been placed on earth and into human form via a series of events.

The three ladies return and I can see Antanov looking toward Christina.

"Yes, they both have similar marks," Christina says.

"So, they could be genuine...or maybe you have all escaped from somewhere?" asks Antanov cheerily, "Maybe that choice of restaurant by Christina wasn't such a random selection. Gogol and all that."

I realise that Antanov is referencing Gogol, the Ukrainian godfather of Russian literature, but I'm not sure whether it is Diary of a Madman or Dead Souls to which he refers.

Awkward, either way.

"We can prove it," says Charlie, "That we have knowledge of the future; not betting odds or anything practical, but that we know, for example, that during a meeting of the UN Human Rights Council, over 100 diplomats will walk out in protest over a speech by Russian foreign minister Sergei Lavrov. The meeting is tomorrow and the scale of the walkout will be unprecedented."

I was thankful that Charlie took an interest in the affairs around the Klima Wars.

"Okay," says Christina, now smiling, "We'll watch the TV broadcast tomorrow. If it happens, you'll be a step closer to credibility."

Antanov looks towards me. He winks. I can sense that he and Christina are now beginning to believe our improbable story.

Hunkt down

"We need to move from here for now though, " says Charlie, "We can go into town,"

"Is that the one I could see from the air?" I ask "Leshkovo?"

"Not quite, we'll be going to Pavlovskaya Sloboda," says Charlie, "I think we'll be off the grid there, whereas in this building there are all kinds of extra wires."

She gestured to us and we all followed her out through a different exit realising the building was large enough to be a corporate headquarters.

"I've found a small place in Pavlovskaya Sloboda, where we should be able to talk without being listened to. I hope you all like Georgian food."

We walked toward a dark silver Range Rover, and only as we climbed in did I realise we were in some kind of Chinese clone car.

"It's a Hunkt Canticie," explained Antanov, "The Chinese have copied the Range Rover Sport externally, but put a whole different interior in."

I looked at the interior, which was all LED displays and reminded my Scrive-brain of a Mercedes.

Charlie is driving as Antanov adds, "It's also all-electric, and only costs about one tenth the amount of a Range Rover equivalent. It's quite popular as a Russian convoy vehicle!"

"I don't remember any of this kind of cloning in the place from which we come," I say. Then I remember that the Chinese were copying the healthcare products that we used. The so-named tropus and the nano-machines. It was big business.

Charlie deftly manœuvres the large vehicle up a slope and around a few sharp bends. We have bright sunshine and I can see that the ground lacks vegetation, presumably from the heat.

"It must be why we were propelled to this time and place," Charlie says, "I mean, we had just staged an Intervention in the future to stop Earth from entering an end-state."

"End-state?" asks Antanov, "You mean like the end of the world?"

"Kinda," continues Charlie, "We could see that the world was running out of resources and that it had suffered from huge losses because of the so-named Klima Wars."

We had reached a main road and Charlie was driving us south-west. I noticed the sign for Павловская Слобода - Pavlovskaya Sloboda - and then a few minutes later we are in the sweeping curves of a quiet town. On both sides of the road are some impressive and bright pastel-coloured onion-towered buildings and I get a proper sense of being in rural Russia.

Charlie slows toward a large blocky-looking building with several rows of large lettering on the outside.

I'm expecting us to be going to somewhere modern and utilitarian and am quite surprised when we climb some stairs to enter a small cosy restaurant, with sweeping curtains, chandeliers and several luscious carpets with varied tables and chairs around them. It reminds me of an overly neat replica of the kind of place I would expect to see in Hoxton, London. I can see outside has a balcony and a view toward the dual carriageway, on which is another one of the onion-tower buildings, this time in a pretty green colour.

We are greeted by a friendly waitress and shown to a corner table with bench seating along one side and loose chairs on the other side.

Charlie announces, "Okay, we can talk here, without being electronically monitored, and I think you'll love the food. So where were we?"

Chantal moves a couple of the cushions and begins, "The thing that comes with any form of Intervention is the prospect of unintended consequences. Like when you buy a new hat but can't see so well because it has a wide brim and then bump into a handsome man on a bicycle."

"Okay, enough from your private life, Chantal," says Charlie.

"But if you are all super-gods, can't you fix all of this anyway?" asks Christina.

"That's just it. We are not. Not super gods. We are entities with long term existences, but with no control over anything. It's a big deal if we 'Intervene' and typically we'd only do this once through all of time," explained Charlie.

"You don't know about Presences and Personas yet, they have not been invented or discovered, but in the future, there will be engineering to produce human-form robotics which can be driven by humanoid Personas. In effect a Presence inhabited by a Persona."

"That's what each of us is emulating. We are three entities placed inside human forms and limited mainly to the sphere of actions of the human. We were each blasted by a Trigax railgun and sent back to this era. Before that we were the same three humans but living in an entirely different version of Earth."

"You have to admit that it sounds far-fetched?" says Antanov, "I mean, time travel, inhabiting other human forms, Trigax rail guns. It sounds like an episode of a Science fiction TV-show."

I realise this is going to be a long haul with the scepticism of Antanov and Christina. If they really are spies or secret agents or similar, then they would be trained to not believe anything they were told.

Christina makes the move, "Okay so we'll suspend disbelief. Tell us what you are attempting to do."

Charlie begins," Well, I was sent back to here and have been connected to the Russian state's security police. It's a massive advantage to you both as you've been tasked by your handler, Blackbird, to get to Putin. I can provide a way for you to get inside the citadel that Putin has constructed, through my links to its physical security management."

Christina adds, "I had other dealings with Putin, indirectly. A friend of mine, Irina, another agent, was linked with him and told me of his time in Dresden. He has a nickname acquired from Dresden when he first arrived in Sankt Petersburg. It was Volodya or 'little Vladimir'. If you look carefully even now, you'll see he wears shoes with 4 cm lifts in them.

"Does that explain why he walks oddly, hardly moving his right arm?" asks Chantal, "I noticed on the TV channels, with so much coverage of him over the last few days."

Antanov and Christina look at one another, then Christina speaks, "No, that's Alpha Team training, " she explains, "When you are trained to a high level in the Russian military, you are taught to adopt 'gunslinger's gait', it's a way to walk that keeps your gun arm close to your side. Watch a group of Russian businessmen and you'll see several of them adopt the same military style. Sometimes it is truly ingrained and other times they are just copying Putin."

"Not a good look, though," says Chantal, "But sorry, Christina, I interrupted you."

Christina continues, "My friend Irina explained that Putin was friendly with the Dresden Stasi and that the Stasi's lieutenant-colonel knew everyone in town. He oversaw organising safe houses and secret apartments for agents and informants, and for procuring goods for the Soviet 'friends'. Putin learned some Stasi tradecraft which he used to such devastating effect in Saint

Petersburg."

"Is that how Saint Petersburg became the home of so much illicit trade?" asked Chantal.

"That's right," answered Christina, "The KGB was recruiting agents in companies like Siemens, Bayer, Messerschmidt and Thyssen. Putin was involved, initially through the Dresden Stasi, but increasingly in his own right. There was a firm called VEB Robotron, which made computers for East Germany right in Dresden. They had to get the plans and parts from the West and lured western businessmen to their offices and beyond."

"Early sleaze and smuggling?" asked Chantal.

"You could say that. Irina was on duty at business meetings in Sankt Petersburg which comprised about ten minutes of business talk followed by a half an hour of discussion of the evening's entertainment. Sometimes Putin and his friends would all drink too much vodka and then reminisce about the old days in Dresden. According to Irina, Putin himself would usually go easy, but everyone else... well. That's when I heard about the blueprint for a lot of Putin's money moves. Irina explained it was a scheme set up by the East German foreign trade ministry. They created the Kommerzielle Koordinierung, with a mission to earn illicit hard currency through smuggling and to bankroll the Stasi acquisition of embargoed technology."

Charlie says, "I've heard of the KoKo, didn't it set up a string of front companies all across Germany, Austria, Switzerland and Liechtenstein?"

"Yes, KoKo answered to the Stasi espionage department

and ran those companies with trusted agents. Some of them had multiple identities, who brought in hard currency through smuggling deals and the sale of illicit arms to the Middle East and Africa."

"I know the feeling with the multiple identities!" smiled Chantal.

"Yes, me too. But back in those days, the Iron Curtain meant that smuggling became the only way for the eastern bloc to keep up with the rapidly developing achievements of the capitalist West," answered Christina.

"And presumably access to a sea-port like Saint Petersburg meant that Putin could develop similar schemes only much larger in scale?" asked Chantal.

"And then some," says Antanov, "Three men held an intimate knowledge of the secret financing systems of the Communist Party at the time the KGB was preparing for the transition to a market economy under Gorbachev's perestroika reforms.

"The innocent sounding Property Department was run by Nikolay Kruchina and Georgy Pavlov. It was thought to have a value of $9 billion although Western experts estimated its foreign holdings at many times more.

"That was because of all the slush funds and the way that money could be marked up and marked down?" asks Chantal

Antanov nods, "But in the first few days after the Communist Party's collapse, Russia's new rulers were surprised to discover that the Party's coffers were nearly empty."

"The money had been shifted offshore. Just like the moves of the oligarchs today. Get caught holding cash and someone will be after it," says Christina.

"Precisely - that's why so many Russians buy London properties and other illiquid assets. They are much harder to 'cash in'," answers Antanov, "At the time the rumours were that Nikolay Kruchina had worked with officials to siphon billions of roubles and other currencies through foreign joint ventures hastily set up in the final years of the regime. These were the filter companies set up in Germany and other countries. It's a move that Putin understood back then but is also using right now."

Christina interrupts, "And Putin used the same moves on his rise to the top. He played it out first in Saint Petersburg, but then carried the book of tricks back to Moscow."

Antanov continues, "Now there were Russian prosecutors investigating what had happened to the Party funds - valued at hundreds of millions of dollars. The institutions Kruchina served were being dismantled in front of his eyes."

"Yeltsin had moved in to break things up?" asked Chantal.

Antanov nods, "Yes, the pro- democratic Russian leader Boris Yeltsin signed a decree, broadcast live, suspending the Soviet Communist Party and ending its decades of rule. It was a big deal. Yeltsin's defiant stance against the hard-line leaders of the attempted coup had put him firmly in the ascendant. "

"Yes, and Yeltsin was going to kick over some tables," says Christina.

"That's right," said Antanov, "Boris Yeltsin by far eclipsed Gorbachev, who timidly watched as Yeltsin addressed the Russian parliament. Arguing that the Communist Party was to blame for the illegal coup, Yeltsin ordered that the sprawling, warren of the Party's Central Headquarters on Moscow's Old Square be sealed."

Christina interrupts, "Putin had been a couple of steps ahead of this. He'd kept all his papers in Dresden and then burned them, along with the papers of others who were later to be his allies."

Antanov says, "That's right, although most of it is impossible to prove, except what Putin boasted on the record about - you know - the furnace exploding from the intensity of the flames."

He continues, "But in Old Square's hundreds of rooms there were filed the secrets of the Soviet Union's vast financial empire, a network that spanned thousands of administrative buildings, hotels, dachas and sanatoriums, as well as the Party's hard-currency bank accounts and untold hundreds, perhaps thousands, of foreign firms set up as joint ventures in the dying days of the regime.

"Through these bank accounts and other connected firms, the strategic operations of the Communist Party abroad – and those of allied political parties had been funded.

"It was the engine room of the Soviet struggle for supremacy against the West. This was the empire that Kruchina had administered as the chief of the Communist Party's property department since 1983. Its sudden sealing felt like a symbol of all that was lost. "

Christina asked, "You know what is coming, don't you?"

"A mysterious disappearance or death of people who know too much?" asked Chantal.

Antanov continues, "Yes, exactly; you know the old KGB moves! Kruchina must have known that his days were numbered. He went back to his flat in the closely guarded compound for the Party elite. Kruchina's wife went to bed leaving her troubled husband alone to sleep on the couch.

"Next morning, she was awoken by a knock on her door. It was the KGB security man for the building. Her husband, she was told, had fallen to his death from the window of their seventh- floor flat."

"Fell or was pushed?" asked Chantal.

Antanov continues, "Yes, you are ahead of us, Chantal. The security man said he'd discovered a crumpled note lying on the pavement next to Kruchina's body. 'I'm not a conspirator,' it said. 'But I'm a coward. Please tell the Soviet people this.' "

"Hmm - a little staged? Why on the pavement? It doesn't ring true." says Chantal.

"Well, the KGB immediately declared his death a suicide. But to this day, no one knows what exactly happened – or if they do, they are not willing to tell," answered Antanov.

"You said three people...Three deaths?" asked Chantal.

"Yes, the same thing happened to Kruchina's predecessor

from the property department. Georgy Pavlov also fell to his death from the window of his flat. It was also recorded as a suicide.

"The same pattern?" asked Chantal.

Antanov continues, "Yes, and then, days after Pavlov's death, another high- ranking member of the Party's financial machine fell to his death from his balcony. This time it was the American Section chief of the Communist Party's international department, Dmitry Lissovolik. Again, it was recorded as a suicide.

Christina adds, "These three all knew about the money – but no-one else knew where it had been hidden. And 'someone' was learning how to cover tracks."

"So somewhere there's a lot of hidden Soviet money in play?" asks Chantal

Buddy house

"I can see where this is leading, " says Chantel, "We're going to infiltrate the oligarch circle to gain access to Putin's inner circle. And Charlie has a property right next door to one of the oligarchs."

"So right now, we need to go to the home of one of Putin's buddies?" asked Antanov, "Isn't that incredibly dangerous?"

"Well, we have several to choose from," says Charlie, "All in a line along the road where we are based. I'm inclined to make it our next-door neighbour. His name is Svalov Rollan Vitalievich and he is a mere civil servant from the construction industry.

"Vitalievich could be said to have his fat fingers in many pies and used this to successfully overcome personal budget crises, as evidenced from the size of his cottage.

"His adjacent plot and home combined are worth approximately 178 million roubles which is around US$5.4 billion. Not bad for a civil servant.

Charlie continues, "I've researched him and Vitalievich

has been head of the Federal State Unitary Enterprise 'Spetsstroyinzhiniring' under the Federal Agency of Special Construction (SpetsStroy Russia). Before that he was head of the Federal State Unitary Enterprise 'Head Department for Road and Airfield Construction of the Federal Agency of Special Construction'.

"That's a wide range of powerful roles," said Antanov.

Charlie says, "Hmm, but even more so when you add on that he is Minister of Regional Development for the Russian Federation and Governor of Krasnoyarsk Krai, as well as a member of the United Russia Party. He helped mastermind the Asia-Pacific Economic Co-operation in Vladivostok."

"Oh yes," says Antanov, "One of the Putin government's most cynical hallmarks is to line its pockets under the cover of increasing Russia's international prestige. Cynically, they, don't even bother to cover it up. Thus, practically every ordinary person you meet will tell you that the Sochi Olympics, the Soccer World Cup, and the APEC Summit served only one purpose: to expropriate and launder state funds."

Antanov continues, "As a mere drop in the ocean, I remember when the government made available an extra $11.2 million to buy 120 brand new luxury BMWs to transport APEC summit guests. The request had previously been rejected by the treasury on the grounds that there are already plenty of limos to ferry visiting dignitaries: the office of the President has over 100 BMW 7 Series, almost 200 5 Series and over 300 luxury Ford Mondeos in its car park. Yet mysteriously the original refusal was somehow quietly overturned. One source cited the need to honour an unspoken rule that visiting dignitaries must travel in brand new cars."

Christina adds, "The more important rule is that once the summit is over, 120 lucky bureaucrats were rewarded for their loyalty with some very nice cars."

Christina added, "There's clearly no need to fish for the obvious parallels between the length of the construction projects overseen by United Russia party member Vitalievich and the size of his estate."

"So, he's the one, then," says Charlie, "Our new friend."

False Flags

We had all ordered from the Georgian Menu. Now an assortment of Georgian foods arrived, ideal for us to share around. Khinkali - A twisted topped Georgian mega-dumpling, Shashlik - skewered cubes of lamb, Khachapuri - an oval of a dough similar to pizza, with cheese and a whole egg served on top. and small bowls of Kharcho soup of beef stock seasoned with garlic, suneli, pepper, chilli, cinnamon, and ajika.

"Charlie, this is so much better than making something in that fancy lobby with the microwave!" says Chantal.

"Yes, it's delicious and very authentic," says Christina, "In Georgia, herbs and crops are cultivated in mountains and valleys, while cattle and sheep are put to pasture. People of Georgia mostly combine these two food groups in their food. Of course, we should really have it with Usakhelauri wine - it's a sweet wine, harvested after the first frost."

Antanov gestured and a bottle of the wine was forthcoming from the waitress.

Charlie refused the wine but continued the

conversation, "We should take a closer look at what is happening today,"

"It seems as if misinformation is becoming the norm," observes Antanov, "My serious concern is that Putin could use chemical weapons on Kyiv as Russian propagandists spread what the US White House press secretary, Jen Psaki has called 'false claims about alleged US biological weapons labs and chemical weapons development in Ukraine'. The Kremlin has produced no evidence to support its Ukranian weapons lab claims, which were called 'preposterous' by Psaki and have been dismissed by Ukraine's government."

"And right now," begins Charlie, "Ukraine's president, Volodymyr Zelensky, has called a Russian strike on a maternity hospital in Mariupol 'the ultimate evidence of genocide'. Zelensky said children were buried under rubble and the regional governor said 17 people were wounded when the hospital was destroyed by a Russian airstrike."

So, things are speeding up," observes Antanov to Charlie, "I guess that makes your initiative more urgent,"

"Our initiative," says Charlie, "You are on the inside now."

We chinked wine glasses and said, "Nah zdorov'ye!"

Chantel continues the conversation, "When I've looked at this time span as a Watcher, it is so difficult to see the nuances. I mean, every report has been manipulated, and right now I can see the Russian news suppression first hand."

Antanov asked, "But surely, if you are really Watchers,

then you would be wise to all of this, not just seeing things through the history books of victors?"

"Yes," says Christina, "You watch a Russian news program and it won't talk about a war. It won't show the atrocities of the sustained bombing of civilians. Most Russians won't even believe it when they hear directly from their children phoning them from Ukraine."

"We really take your point, but I'm not sure we are ever normally as close to a conflict as on this occasion," I answer.

Antanov looks at me, "Normal Russian civilians don't know that there has been a sustained exodus of millions of refugees fleeing Ukraine. Some 2.5 million people have already fled, according to the United Nations, which calls it Europe's fastest-growing refugee crisis since 1945. More than half are now in Poland but tens of thousands are also staying in Moldova and Bulgaria, which have some of the fastest shrinking populations."

Christina continues, "It's like the Syrian civil war in that it has the possibility to continue for years. In that war, international organisations have accused virtually all sides involved, including the Ba'athist Syrian government, ISIL, opposition rebel groups, Russia, Turkey, and the U.S.-led coalition. All of them accused of severe human rights violations and massacres.

Antanov speaks, "The Syrian conflict caused a major refugee crisis, with millions fleeing to neighbouring Turkey, Lebanon and Jordan. Even with the number of peace initiatives launched, the fighting continued. And it suffers from war fatigue now, with few reports because of its length and the selective blindness that the world suffers for certain trouble spots and ethnicities."

Charlie adds, "They say something about history repeating itself, but I'd add a filter of ethnicity and culturalism. Like the British conveniently burying most of the slave trade, except for William Wilberforce, the abolitionist.

Christina adds, "I know, even the inventor of Newspeak, George Orwell, once likened Britain to a wealthy family that maintains a guilty silence about the sources of its wealth.

Charlie agrees, "Orwell, the author of 1984, whose real name was Eric Blair, had seen the conspiracy of silence at close quarters. His father, Richard W Blair, was a civil servant who oversaw the production of opium on plantations near the Indian-Nepalese border for export to China.

She continued, "The department for which the elder Blair worked was called the opium department. The Blair family fortune – which had been lost by the time Eric was born – stemmed from their investments in plantations far from India. Wilberforce's Slavery Abolition Act freed 800,000 Africans who were then the legal property of Britain's slave owners.

Christina adds, "What is less well known is that the same act contained a provision for the financial compensation of the slave owners through a £20 million government pay-off. That's £17 billion in today's money. The largest bailout in British history until the banks in 2008."

News Management from Russia, echoing the Newspeak of Orwell's 1984, plus financial compensation to assist cover selective memories, of events quietly erased from history.

Georgian food and wine

We'd eaten the feast of Georgian food and were all looking slightly relaxed around the table. I wondered if it was the Usakhelauri wine.

"And so, to the next event which I will be managing," explains Charlie, "Scrive, it will be great to have you along, to help Antanov and I sniff out any trouble."

"And me?" asked Chantal.

"Oh, you'll add your stylish and disarming presence," smiled Charlie.

"What's the reason for a meeting?" I ask.

Charlie answers, "Vitalievich has called a meeting of his fellow oligarchs. Tellingly, in this group of Putin's followers there's no one directly linked to Putin's inner circle. This group are all worried about the extreme drop in value of their wealth since Putin started his war against Ukraine."

Antanov comments, "Yes then rouble is 20% lower than before Putin started his military action and Gazprom shares have gone from US$8.50 to about US$0.58 since the start of February. No wonder the oligarchs want to talk."

Christina adds, "But I guess that most of these people have diversified their holdings? It is probably spread around property portfolios and multiple currencies?"

"But do we know who the real inner circle comprises?" I ask.

Charlie answers, "Well, we shouldn't underestimate any of the people that Vitalievich has asked, but they are nowadays all a step away from the true inner circle. The inner guard are the people best able to advise Putin whilst he is on a war footing. They are the ones we ultimately need to get to. But we need to use this outer group to get to the inner ones."

Wheels within wheels.

Christina starts, "I think Antonov and I know more about the inner circle. Vladimir Putin cuts a solitary figure, leading Russia's military into a high-risk war that threatens to tear apart his country's economy. Russians are not allowed to call it a war though - it's a 'Special Military Operation'. Putin has rarely looked more isolated than in two recent, choreographed appearances with his inner circle, where he sits at a resolute and some would say ridiculous distance from his closest advisers."

Christina adds, "There's his long-time confidant Sergei Shoigu, who has parroted the Putin line of demilitarising Ukraine and protecting Russia from the West's so-called military threat. This is a man who goes on hunting and fishing trips with the president to Siberia, and he has in the past been viewed as a potential successor.

She continues, "Shoigu has a previous track record. He was labelled with the military seizure of Crimea in 2014. He was also in charge of the GRU military intelligence agency, accused of two nerve agent poisonings - the deadly 2018 attack in Salisbury in the UK and the near-fatal attack on opposition leader Alexei Navalny in Siberia in 2020. One could say he is a nasty piece of work.

"Shoigu is not only in charge of the military, but also partly in charge of ideology - and in Russia ideology is mostly about history and he's in control of the narrative."

Then Antanov speaks, "Valery Gerasimov is Chief of General Staff of the Russian Armed Forces. As chief of staff, it is his job to invade Ukraine and complete the job fast, and by that standard he has been found wanting.

"He has played a major role in Vladimir Putin's military campaigns ever since he commanded an army in the Chechen War of 1999, and he was at the forefront of military planning for Ukraine too, overseeing military drills in Belarus last month.

Christina adds, "He is the one who describes hacking the enemy's society, rather than direct head-on attack."

Antonov grimaces, "That's not the way it is running in Ukraine, though. Gerasimov is described as a "humourless bruiser" and played a key role in the military campaign to annexe Crimea."

Christina adds, "Some reports suggest Gerasimov has now been sidelined because of the stuttering start to the invasion of Ukraine and reports of poor morale among the troops because of the under-provided logistics, like no fuel for the tanks as well as food shortages."

Antanov continues, "Nikolai Patrushev, Secretary of the Security council, is the most hawkish hawk, thinking the West has been out to get Russia for years. He is one of three Putin loyalists who have served with him ever since the 1970s in St Petersburg, when Russia's second city was still known as Leningrad. Few hold as much influence over the president as Nikolai Patrushev. Not only did he work with Putin in the old KGB during the communist era, but he also replaced Putin as head of its successor organisation, the FSB, from 1999 to 2008."

Christina adds, "It was during a bizarre meeting of Russia's security council, three days before the Ukraine invasion, that Mr Patrushev pushed his view that the US's concrete goal was the break-up of Russia."

The session was an example of FSB theatre, showing the president holding court behind a desk as each of his security team walked up to a lectern and expressed their opinion on recognising the independence of Russian-backed rebels in Ukraine. It had clearly been edited before it was broadcast, to remove most, but not all, of the mistakes.

Patrushev passed the test. Antonov explains, "He's the one who has the chief battle cry, and there's a sense in which Putin has moved towards his more extreme position."

Antanov adds, "The other two stalwarts are security service chief Alexander Bortnikov (Director of the Federal Security Service - FSB and Director of the Foreign Intelligence Service (SVR) Sergei Naryshkin."

Christina speaks, "All the president's inner circle are known as siloviki, or 'enforcers', but this trio of

Patrushev, Bortnikov and Naryshkin are closer still.

"Kremlin watchers say the president trusts information he receives from the security services more than any other source, and Alexander Bortnikov is seen as being part of the Putin inner sanctum. Bortnikov is another old hand from the Leningrad KGB and took over the leadership of its replacement FSB when Nikolai Patrushev moved on.

Antanov add, "Completing the trio of old Leningrad spooks, Sergei Naryshkin has remained alongside the president for much of his career. What, then, should we make of a remarkable dressing down he was subjected to when he went off-message during the security council meeting? When asked for his assessment of the situation, the intelligence chief became flustered and fluffed his lines, only to be told by the president: 'That's not what we're discussing.' The lengthy session was edited so the Kremlin had clearly decided to show his discomfort in front of a big television audience.

"It was shocking. He's incredibly cool and collected so people will have asked what's going on here although Putin loves playing games with his inner circle, making Naryshkin look a fool."

Christina explained, "Sergei Naryshkin has long shadowed Putin, in St Petersburg in the 1990s, then in Putin's office in 2004 and eventually becoming speaker of parliament. He is also a historian and provides the president with ideological grounds for his actions. He also gets sent out by Putin to issue denials about poisonings, cyber-attacks, and election interference.

Antanov's turn: "Sergei Lavrov, 71, is yet more proof that Vladimir Putin heavily relies on figures from his past.

For 18 years he has been Russia's most senior diplomat, presenting Russia's case to the world even if he is not considered to have a big role in decision-making. He is a wily operator who attempted to ridicule British Foreign Secretary Liz Truss over Russian geography and the year before sought to humiliate the EU's foreign policy chief.

"But he has long been sidelined on anything to do with Ukraine and, despite his gruff and hostile reputation, he advocated further diplomatic talks on Ukraine and the Russian president chose to ignore him.

Christina adds, "Then we get to Valentina Matviyenko. She is another Putin loyalist from St Petersburg who helped steer through the annexation of Crimea in 2014 as well. A rare female face in the Putin entourage, she oversaw the upper house's vote to rubber stamp the deployment of Russian forces abroad, paving the way for invasion.

"But she is not considered to be a primary decision-maker. That said, few people can say with complete certainty who is calling the shots and taking the big decisions. Just like every other member of Russia's security council, her role was to give an impression of a collective discussion when it is more than likely the Russian leader had already made up his mind."

Wealth erosion

We'd all enjoyed the Georgian food, now the restaurant hosts returned with a bottle of almost clear liquid. I sensed immediately that this could be dangerous.

Christina and Antanov laugh, "Oh yes, you must try this. Chacha - wine brandy, or sometimes called vodka brandy – It's made with the remains of the grapes after the wine has been extracted."

"They say you should only drink it when you are already drunk," explains Antonov, "And unsurprisingly it often gets sold in plastic bottles."

"But this is the good stuff," explains Christina, "Askaneli Premium in a glass bottle. Only about 45% alcohol."

"Maybe I'll pass," says Chantal.

"And me," says Charlie, "I'm driving."

"The rest of you should let a sip of this devil's liquid cross your lips," says Christina, "to protect from evil."

The waiter had already poured a small quantity into an

array of shot glasses.

All of us except Charlie tried it and I had that little stab in my head which was my first warning that things could get messy. It reminded me of Italian grappa. Not normally something I'd swig in large quantities.

Fortunately, Charlie starts talking again, "I've been asked to run the security, along with a few from the GRU and, as of now, with my own associates."

I saw Christina look at Antanov. I wonder if they were both concerned that they would be recognised.

"I know what you are thinking," says Christina to me, "but we've had our great co-incidence with Antanov and me working together again. I don't think we'll run into anyone else from our days at FSB and GRU."

"Well, there is one other big co-incidence," says Antanov, "I knew the police investigator who investigated the Ozero Dacha Co-operative. He worked for Sankt Petersburg's major case squad reporting to a round table of European prosecutors in Sofia.

"This cop knew everything about Putin, all the nitty-gritty, all the cases from the early 1990s, the ties with organised crime, the origins of the Ozero Dacha Co-op, and how nearly its entire membership later migrated to the board of Rossiya Bank.

Antanov continues, "The cop ran the investigation of the Twentieth Trust Corporation, unofficially dubbed the Putin case. As an example, Putin was investigated for a deal he oversaw while he was an official in the mayor's office. The deal involved the export of $100m worth of raw materials in exchange for food for the citizens of St

Petersburg. It was all well documented at the time. The materials were exported, but the food never arrived. Of course, the case was shut down when Putin became President, and the investigator was put out to pasture. Let's just say that Putin seemed to acquire a pretty Spanish villa around that time."

Christina adds, "It is all a criminal conspiracy of greedy, unprincipled liars who will not baulk at any trick or power play to increase their dominion and grab more money, land, oil companies, yachts, real estate, and other goodies. It is the same thing with Russia's completely non-existent 'senate.' Russia's upper house of parliament is called the Federation Council, and its members are rubber stampers, not 'senators,' but that was what they took to calling themselves a few years ago, and so nowadays almost everyone calls them that, too.

She continued, "But they are not senators, if only because there is no senate in Russia. More to the point, Russia's un-senators are well-connected, highly paid sock puppets of Putin's Kremlin.

"Likewise, a perpetual, self-replicating mafia dictatorship runs with sovereign wastefulness, major league legal anarchy, hyper-corruption, and sheer absurdity. The Putin regime is an improvised exercise in radical governance by former KGB officers and their gangster friends.

Antanov speaks again, "Putin's public support of democracy was a put-on when he worked as Petersburg Mayor Anatoly Sobchak's deputy in the early 1990s. Then he was the Saint Petersburg bag man. Nowadays, he has moved up in the world considerably, but basically not changed his profession."

Sam's in the car park

We all return to Charlie's hideaway, with Charlie driving us there in the Range-Rover clone. Charlie is first on the phone and then prepares to visit the adjacent property where Vitalievich lives.

"Can you come along?" she asks Antanov. It will be good to have someone clearly from 'inside the business' who can help me scope the place. We'll be best to save Scrive for another day."

"Sure, I'll ride shotgun," says Antanov, smiling as Charlie prepares for the short drive to the adjacent property.

"Are you taking a weapon?" asks Christina, "Only they will be bound to search you."

"Yes, I'll take a polymer pistol, something like a Zastava PPZ," said Antanov. It will make them think but illustrate that my weaponry is Russian influenced."

"Serbian," said Christina, "just like the M70 Kalashnikov."

"Okay, don't worry about us," said Charlie, "I've been highly recommended to Vitalievich. Our aim is to be along for the big talks between the Ozero community."

I watched Charlie and Antanov stroll out of the exit, on their way to setting up what I was starting to regard as our infiltration of the outer circle.

**

Two days later and the stage is set for Vitalievich's meeting with the rest of the oligarchs. Charlie has been briefed by Vitalievich and his on-site security team. It was a strange setup. Vitalievich was wary of infiltration, but also of incursions from a Russian mafia gang and even from Putin's own inner circle.

Now we had the oligarchs from the rest of the Ozero Community and a few of their trusted friends together in a room. Charlie was running the front security and Vitalievich's own people were acting more of less as simple bodyguards.

It was fascinating to watch. Charlie had managed to put the fear of an attempt on any or all of them into their minds and the team was looking very nervous.

I knew that Charlie had created elaborate ring defences around Vitalievich's property and that it included a Patriot MIM-104 SAM Surface-to-Air missile launcher with had been parked in our own adjacent property.

"Where did you get that?" I ask Antanov.

"It's amazing how much of this equipment is available on the black market," he answered, "Think about it, these were designed in 1969, and are still in production today. Raytheon has manufactured over 10,000 of the missiles in that time, and that excludes any clones that have been created. They are so much easier to use than the Russian S-400 because they don't need to be networked to an AWAC plane to work. These Patriots can be driven into position, parked and primed. It is very useful if we think there is anything incoming hostile."

I was still intrigued where Antanov was getting these expensive pieces of kit. First a helicopter and now a truckload of surface-to-air missiles. Blackbird must be bankrolling him. I noticed him adding in coordinates too, of each of the Ozero Community dachas. I wondered why he'd do this unless he was saving the coordinates for a rainy day.

The trusted people Charlie wanted in the meeting room were herself, me, and Christina. Chantal was to run comms from our building next door and Antanov was to be outside close to the SAM launcher and a small team which operated it. These extra personnel arrived in a Bumerang armoured personnel carrier, which Christina had marvelled was the latest state of the art vehicle of the Russian Army.

Christina designated a sheltered spot outside Vitalievich's building as a pick-up point if there was trouble. Antanov was to use the APC as an unlikely getaway vehicle.

Antanov wasn't using Budget-Rent-a-Car to get this equipment, but it still seemed to come easily to him. I wondered how threatened his connections must be to resort to this level of bankrolling.

Vitalievich's own security detail were to stay around him but seem to only have handguns for protection and rudimentary airline-level security systems. They were blissfully unaware of the high technology equipment in the next property.

The first of the visitors arrive and Vitalievich's security detail run entry scanners to check that everyone was unarmed. Every major attendee seems to bring around four additional people in their entourage.

Soon we had a roomful of people comprising the United Russia Party friends of Svalov Rollan Vitalievich.

Notables include Nikolay Ivanovich Ashlapov, Igor Nikolayevich Rudensky, Sergey Eduardovich Prikhodko and Vyacheslav Viktorovich Volodin. Additional attendees include Nikolay Sergeevich Shustenko, President of the Bazis group of companies, Miller MacMillan, President of Raven Holdings and Tsarsko Adam Borisovich from Mirovyye Aktivy.

Altogether, we have approximately 50 people in the meeting room, with 8 main contacts and around 30 assistants, plus our own security detail.

If anyone had wanted to neutralise this gathering, then they would create a large hole in the United Russia Party. I could see how Charlie was earning the big bucks and could source a SAM system to provide protection.

Then it is time for Vitalievich to start the meeting.

Out of his mind

We arranged the meeting room to have an inner table where the eight main guests could sit, with one assistant each to take notes. Alongside Vitalievich sat a couple of other presenters. Behind them all were seated the other folk, who we assumed were the protection and heavies.

It did make the room look kind of comical, with the second row filled with mainly bruisers in their leather jackets, with the glitter of heavy chain jewellery.

"Straight from central casting," whispered Chantal, into my earpiece. She had watched from outside as the various people arrived, in mainly large grey, black, or silver SUVs. I noticed that several the vehicles had blue lights mounted on them.

Christina had taken a control position in one corner of the room, and I instinctively knew where I should take up position, guided by Scrive's instincts.

That left Charlie, in a blue and grey combat outfit, to roam free which attracted stares from many of the security row. She was dressed in an ironic choice of colours, echoing NATO uniform, which Putin was anxious to keep out of Ukraine and away from the Russian borders.

Vitalievich opens the meeting and looks over to his small group of other presenters. He asks Dr Maria Gvasalia, a psychologist from M.V. Lomonosov Moscow State University, to step forward.

Vitalievich explains, "Dr Gvasalia is a Psychological Practitioner who has a background in political psychology and has done extensive work on psychology and political identities including that of President Putin. She speaks as news that Russian forces bombed a maternity hospital in Mariupol in Ukraine, killing three people - including a child - and injuring at least 17 others."

This was a departure from the party line. To comment as if Russia was in a war was strictly forbidden in Russia and carried a 15-year prison sentence. I guess Vitalievich has done it to help Dr Gvasalia trust the rooms attendees.

I can see Christina and Charlie checking out the expressions on the faces of the leather men.

Christina breathes into my earpiece, "There's one guy, shoulder length dark hair, small silver lapel badge of a Russian flag, sitting behind Volodin, who looks startled by that last statement. He's also sweating and looks as if he might make a move."

Dr Maria Gvasalia pulled no punches, "President Vladimir Putin has been widely accused of war crimes after intense shelling of civilian areas since his military invasion of Ukraine has met with increasingly stiff resistance from Ukrainian forces."

"Putin is one who manifests what we psychologists would call the Dark Triad,"

I knew about the dark triad from Scrive's brain. It was standard training in his line of work.

Gvasalia started a slide show, in Russian. It said:

Vladimir Putin psychological profile: A psychopath who is likely to get emotional payoffs from Russia's bloodshed in Ukraine, plus, possible impact of his rumoured illness or cancer, including the potential side effects from overdosing on steroids.

Wow. That was quite a slide. I wondered whether Gvasalia had brought her own extra supply of bodyguards. She certainly would not be able to say this kind of thing in public, here in Russia.

Then she went on to explain: "We use discourse analysis to analyse his interviews, his discourse, and the rhetoric that he uses. It is because we are not in a clinical situation with him.

"What he does is demonstrate a high level of control and what is generally known as sociopathy or psychopathy. This psychopathic nature that he manifests is not a clinical term but an umbrella term that has been utilised to almost integrate several personality traits."

One of Vitalievich's invited guests stood.

"This is treason that we are all talking here. I am uncomfortable that if someone leaks this information, then we are all finished. What guarantees can you give us that we are safe to continue this meeting?"

Vitalievich answers, "It amounts to trust. You all know one another and have been to each other's parties and family occasions.

"Today we are building a new Bratva. A new fellowship among the eight. The Восьмерка, the Vos'merka. We have no choice in this matter. We know that Putin has been systematically replacing us with newer people. And that we hold in the palm of our hands a significant amount of the Russian economy. Dr Maria Gvasalia will explain to you all that Putin is ruthless. He has assembled us here in these wealthy compounds, not just as a place to show our riches, but as a wrapped prison compound too."

Maria Gvasalia continues, "The Dark Triad includes three traits: -

- Psychopathic traits: - 'The killer' who wants to control everything around them as belonging to them
- Dark narcissism: Someone who sees himself almost as the most powerful individual on earth
- Machiavellianism: People who are very focussed on the manipulation of people's emotions

"Putin demonstrates a lack of conscience. There is no sense of right and wrong. There is absolutely no remorse in his behaviour, it is about power and control - what is mine is mine and what is yours is mine also. Psychopaths have this overly possessive trait of power and - the psychology of evil - because the more blood they shed the more psychological and emotional payoffs they get. They thrive on murder, killings, and genocide. And this reinforces the behaviour to do more."

Dr Gvasalia adds: "Psychopaths are not necessarily killers - you can also see them in the boardroom, they are controlling and powerful people, who think, 'Look at me, I am more important than you.' In layman's terms you may see them in everyday life, often described as ruthless, people who just don't care about others and abuse others, but a key characteristic is also that they are charming. They will charm and groom and become political or sexual predators driven by evil desires."

She adds, "With Putin you are looking at the fragmentation of his childhood and his background in the KGB. There was a lot of consternation about who his biological father was. He was bullied an awful lot at school and had a low stature.

"Putin's father was a metal worker but he had an amazing respect for the old Soviet Union and communism and believed in the common people - this was Putin's political ideology and he felt this was going to be his life.

"Putin was a loner as a child and the way you survive when bullied for years is you become very aggressive and so there is impulsivity and aggression as a child. He wanted to have power and so he felt allegiance to the KGB and becoming a KGB officer would be a way to demonstrate his feelings for the Russian ideology of communism. Becoming a senior KGB officer would have given him a powerful nature of control. Here you can see his genetics very much interacting with a Soviet ideology and it was this that really began to anchor his identity as an aggressive leader who will fight to preserve Soviet ideology.

"He wants to go back to those days and bring Russia back into the old Soviet economy. However, he says opinion polls show this is not what increasing numbers of Russians want and he believes that younger Russians who want international acceptance will turn on him."

Dr Gvasalia looks around the room. I could see the inner eight nodding in agreement, but a more mixed reception from the leather heavies.

The same challenger stands up again, I've worked out it is Tsarsko Adam Borisovich from Mirovyye Aktivy, "I accept what Vitalievich said earlier, about our need to survive and that as a new Bratva of eight we could wield significant power. But I guess it will depend what Vladimir Putin decides to do next?"

Dr Gvasalia answers, "We must respect military intelligence and what our military leaders know about Putin and his personality. But Putin is not going to be upset by economic sanctions. He will call in some of his war chest of money and anyway has a huge run rate of cashflow from the raw materials that Russia exports. Finland, Germany and Poland can't just stop consuming Russian energy and it would take many months before those sanctions would bite."

"No, for Putin, the challenge is that his identity is under threat and he knows Ukraine could win. Putin is not a man for intergroup conflict discussions or negotiations. See those distant tables he sets for visitors. Any peace deal would have to be on Putin's terms - not Ukrainian premier Zelensky's. If Putin, as a cornered rat, doesn't get his way he will not be going into discussions."

"He tells that story about how hard a cornered rat fights!" says Vitalievich.

"I know, he tells it to everyone, he behaves like a man

under threat the whole time," says Gvasalia, "But now, the irony is that he is increasingly threatened by his own people who don't want either Putin or war. He is having to suppress the news about the protests and to lock up dissenters. He has been successful at this, but the fact that even with news suppression many Russians are beginning to get nervous about his actions, suggests that this is going to be a protracted war between two ideologies of the minds. He is threatened very much by President Zelensky - a highly intelligent guy who wants to protect Ukraine."

"If pushed into a corner to negotiate due to losing ground militarily he will think it reasonable to look at more desperate options, in terms of nuclear, chemical or biological attacks.

"Because he knows economic sanctions are penetrating the whole Russian framework he may threaten: 'I have nuclear power and I will use it.' You will get threat upon threat upon threat: 'I am the most powerful man on earth.'

Gvasalia adds, "I don't think he will use nuclear powers. He is highly impulsive and unpredictable so he could do it but I don't think he will because he will see the aftermath of massive destruction and genocide. It would destroy the entire political framework of Russia. It would also trigger a militaristic strategy against Russia - and nobody wants to see that."

I think forward through history and I still can't remember the sequence of the Klima Wars. I know it created a massive destruction of the Earth's ecosystem, and for a time Earth was on the edge of destruction. I will need to ask Chantal and Charlie what they remember after this meeting concludes. It all feels so distant, like we are in a different universe.

Gvasalia continues, "Putin accepts, like some psychopaths, that if they are going to lose, so must everyone else. Like a child upturning the board in a game of checkers. An extreme attack is more of a possibility than some people might think. Threat is a massive characteristic of his personality but at the end of the day I don't think he will resort to a zero sum game – all or nothing - because he depends too much on oil and gas.

"The whole thing about Putin is that he will want to preserve the way he believes Russia should be. And he will persist and will drive forward his model of the Russia he wants people to adhere to."

Now, Vitalievich interrupts, "We can see that Putin is playing psychopathic tactics, which will hurt all of us, and all the Russian people. I want us to consider the options for bringing him down."

I look instinctively toward the leather-clad security man that Christina identified. He appears to be looking at Tsarsko Adam Borisovich, as if waiting for a signal. Borisovich asked the 'treason' question earlier and I can see that he is much younger than Vitalievich's other invited guests. I remember what Christina said about the young guys pushing the old men out of the windows in Putin's early Kremlin days.

Gvasalia continues, "There could be the influence of his own war cabinet. I believe there could be other militaristic people in his war cabinet who may see things very differently to him. There are also many younger politicians who would be wanting to subscribe to a new contemporary Russia and they will want to usurp him in one way or another. He will feel threatened by them. He knows his days are numbered now; he is in his late sixties now."

Maybe a military coup, a putsch? I just can't remember what sparked the Klima Wars. Although I also can't see Putin taking part in some sort of conflict resolution.

My shaky knowledge of this period means I can't even remember what happened to Putin. I remember there was speculation about cancer. That led to the view about his condition being exacerbated by the use of steroids. The so called 'roid rage.

Gvasalia continues, "He will realise there is going to come a time when he is going to have to hand over the reins. The problem here is that he must do it or someone will take over without his consent. That will terrify him and could exacerbate his cancer. His rivals for leadership may be more complacent and contemporary and he doesn't want that unless they have a similar personality to him. He will know which of his war cabinet would carry on his vision into the future - the same old fashioned soviet personality and identity will be his goal from any successor."

I realise that this creates many contradictions. Putin wanting to reinstate his version of old Russia, although many around him against this.

Maybe a new guard which he has created now starting to have their own different vision.?

Some that he trusts are now in their seventies and may not be useful to his cause for much longer. A citizenship living under his misinformation believing one thing which is becoming increasingly difficult to manipulate.

The same citizenship sceptical of his Soviet values.

Then it happens.

Chatter

The leather clad man that Christina identified suddenly stands. He looks toward Tsarsko Adam Borisovich, who nods, "Da. Do it!"

He points a pistol towards Vitalievich. Before he has a chance to fire it, I notice Borisovich has pulled an identical pistol which is also pointed towards Vitalievich.

I hear a metallic chatter for maybe two seconds. It is considerably quieter and deeper than I'd expected. I'm surprised to see the leather clad man and Borisovich reel backwards. Two other of Borisovich's security detail immediately raise their hands into the air.

"нет проблемы! Не нам. net problemy! Ne nam. No Problem, not us!" yells the first one. Charlie has moved around the room to provide cover across all the seated people.

Christina has a smoking sub machine gun in her hand. She speaks, "Are we done?" she asks, "Anyone else?"

It's clear that the other Russians were surprised by the sudden deadly action. None of them, not even the hardest looking men are prepared for a fight and instead mildly place their hands on their heads.

Vitalievich steps forward, "You were right, Christina. It was Borisovich that wanted to disrupt us. I don't think this was the manner he intended. Thank you for saving my life."

He looked around the table.

"Gentlemen, ladies, I think we should adjourn for an hour so that we can tidy up."

One of Vitalievich's security is already on a phone to bring in a cleaning team. I look across to Dr Maria Gvasalia, who seems un-phased by the whole event.

Vitalievich announces, "When we reconvene, it will be in the ballroom. I will have it arranged like this room. Only for less people. Meanwhile, come through to my cocktail bar. We are serving Champagne - and Beluga caviar, naturally!"

I am mildly shocked by the matter of factness with which the events of the last few minutes are being treated. I speak quietly to Dr Gvasalia, who says, "This is gangland Russia, you should expect such events."

Then I ask Christina how she had known. "It was their chairs, they looked slightly different. They had been substituted by ones that each held a weapon. But frankly their Makarovs were no match for my Sig Sauer SMG. Vitalievich was lucky though; they both hesitated. I think the security guy was waiting for the command from Borisovich."

Will this get reported?" I ask,

"Of course not," says Christina, "They will want to keep quiet a failed assassination attempt along Oligarch Row. And advertising it would only increase the risk of another attempt by someone wanting to make a name for themselves."

Can't remember

I go outside to check in briefly with Chantal. She is with Antanov. They have both been listening in on the secure channel which Charlie set up. I ask Chantal if she can remember what happened to start the Klima Wars, but she doesn't know either.

"It's as if I can't remember this part of 'history' she says. I know I've been through it as a Watcher, but it is as if it doesn't exist. Like I'm in a different version of reality."

"Could it be that we are experiencing it directly, so it seems kind of different?" I ask.

"I wondered that too, but I think I'm being blocked," answers Chantal, "Usually if I spin a little chaos around something I can see its central theme, but not this time. And another thing. Have you noticed the pets around here?"

I shake my head, Pets? Has Chantal lost it?

"I've noticed that cats and dogs seem to be on the wrong scale. Most cats are about the size of a lamb, and dogs, even small ones, seem to go up to the size of a sheep."

As if on cue, a house cat parades across the yard where we are both standing. I look at it closely. It could be a small wildcat. Something like a lynx.

"I think they are just keeping exotic animals as pets," I say, "Some kind of fashion thing."

"Oh yes, and the green sky," she adds, "I could imagine a kind of Aurora Borealis effect in the evening, but we seem to have unnaturally large amounts of green sky."

I realise I'd got used to a green tinge to everything. I assumed that we were in parts of Russia with unpredictable levels of pollution.

"Are you sure it's not an effect of pollution?" I ask, or maybe something washing in from China?"

Perhaps," says Chantal, "But remember I specialise in chaos and there's several tell-tale signs at the moment. Animals, sky, even the power sockets have an unexpected uniformity."

"Chantal!" I say. I'm thinking she has gone strangely obsessive, but then I remember that power sockets were different in different parts of the world. They have suddenly all become like little isosceles triangles and are smaller than I remember.

"Chantal, I think you are reading too much into all of this!"

She smiles, shrugs her shoulders and I can see she is concentrating on the communication equipment again.

Restart

Vitalievich is ready to resume the meeting. Charlie has checked the room and asks me to run over it for a second opinion. We re-vet everyone entering and Christina performs weapon checks, which some of the heavies find entertaining.

This time, Christina makes a point of keeping her copper-coloured Sig Sauer sub-machine gun on display as people enter the room. They take up similar positions around the new table, which pointedly doesn't have space where Borisovich and his crew had sat.

Vitalievich opens the discussion, "Could an assassin kill Putin? Just as the second world war would not have happened without the demonic will and agency of Adolf Hitler, so the invasion of Ukraine – and its horrific bloodshed and unspeakable human misery – is Putin's war. Can he be stopped? The bad news is that the chances do not look good at the moment."

I see people around the table shaking their heads. I expect the oligarchs to be better informed than the security guards, but soon realise that everyone knows the same story of the failing and ever more separate war.

Vitalievich continues, "I want us to consider options to get into his secure location. Putin is protected 24/7 by one of the world's strongest security details, who have sealed him in a closed bubble. All access to him is strictly – almost manically – controlled, in much the same way as it was for Stalin and Hitler.

"The chances of a lone outside assassin like Fanny Kaplan getting to the dictator are zero. Kaplan was a Jewish Ukrainian woman, who, in 1918, fired three bullets into the Bolshevik leader Lenin, outside the Hammer and Sickle factory in Moscow. It sparked a series of strokes that crippled and eventually killed the Soviet dictator."

The point is not lost on this group that a determined assassin could still get close enough to Vitalievich to be able to almost pop two shots toward him.

He adds, "If Putin is to be stopped, ousted, and arrested, or assassinated, the authors of such an attempt will have to come from within the clique who surround him. Desperate times spawn desperate remedies, and only when the clique think that their own futures are directly imperilled by Putin's increasingly dangerous actions are they likely to act."

I consider that it is even difficult for this clique to sift for the truth because so much of what has happened is hidden under a blanket of misinformation. Only indirectly, through the effects on sales of goods and share prices, will many Russians even be aware of the war being waged in their name.

Vitalievich continues, "Putin has already publicly humiliated members of his inner circle by berating them when they have raised the mildest of questions about his actions. They cannot have much affection for this supremely unlovable man. But will their growing doubts about him overcome their fears for their own futures?

"History is replete with examples of successful assassinations carried out by the intimates of dictatorial rulers. Julius Caesar was killed by members of the Roman Senate; numerous Roman emperors like Caligula were murdered by their Praetorian guards, and at least one – Claudius – was probably poisoned by his own wife Agrippina."

Vitalievich could see that he was losing people with these older historical references, so he shifted gear, "Then, in more modern times, King Faisal of Saudi Arabia was killed in 1975 by his own nephew, while India's prime minister Mrs Indira Gandhi was gunned down in 1984 by her Sikh bodyguards, outraged by her attack on their holy Golden Temple in Amritsar."

I could see where this was leading. Vitalievich wanted to find some of these oligarchs who would be prepared to attempt an assassination.

Vitalievich continues, "Nearing the end of his thirty-year rule, a sick and ageing Stalin had become so psychotic that he had arrested and was torturing his own doctors on suspicion of poisoning him and was threatening the lives of his cronies and colleagues in the Soviet Politburo.

"It is said that one of them, the Chief of the Soviet secret police and security services, Lavrenti Beria, acted ruthlessly to save his own skin by actually poisoning his boss – appropriately enough with rat poison warfarin – triggering the stroke that ended Stalin's dreadful life on 5 March 1953. Beria himself proudly boasted of the deed, telling his comrades: 'I did him in! I saved all your lives!'

Vitalievich asserts, "When all decision making has been concentrated in the hands of a single all-powerful ruler, such as Putin, only the physical removal of the tyrant can end the tyranny and lift the danger that he is posing. But perhaps we should be careful what we wish for. Lenin's death as a long-term consequence of Fanny Kaplan's gun shots paved the way for the rise to supreme power of Vladimir Putin's role model, Joseph Stalin."

I thought back through history and recalled an event that was possibly more pertinent to President Putin in his current circumstances. It was the successful killing of Tsar Paul I at St Michael's Castle in St Petersburg in March 1801.

The increasingly eccentric and isolated Tsar had alienated the circle of military and civil officials surrounding him by his erratic foreign policy decisions. Their discontent culminated in a conspiracy which ended with them entering Tsar Paul I's apartment and strangling him. He was succeeded by his son Alexander I who eventually ended the alliance with Napoleon and brought the rampaging French emperor down.

So, if the close circle of Generals and corrupt yes men on whom Putin's power rests are sufficiently alarmed by the increasingly chaotic course of the Ukraine war and the world's horrified reaction to it, is there the faintest chance that they will take a leaf from the playbook of Beria and Tsar Paul's officials and end the crisis by bumping off their boss?

That was precisely the question that Vitalievich was asking he oligarchs in the room.

Vitalievich asks, "As the options open to the those who Putin has protected and promoted begin to close down, and the rage of the Russian people themselves rise, the best hope for ending this crisis may well rest with bad men acting to bring down the still worse and possibly deranged dictator who is leading them and Russia into the abyss.

"To play Putin's own story of 'the rat fights back' against himself, he says he learned a valuable lesson about power in his youth when he cornered a rat in the apartment block where he grew up. Instead of submitting, the rat leapt at his face and attacked him. Now, it is time for the rats in the Kremlin to learn the same lesson and to attack Putin himself."

Vitalievich was trying to incite an assassination of Putin. Whether successful or not, I was stunned that I could not recall this from my Watcher's knowledge of history.

At precisely this moment, a text message arrives on several of the phones in the room. It is captioned from the Kremlin and reads:

"We, the Russian people will always be able to distinguish true patriots from scum and traitors and will simply spit them out like a gnat that accidentally flew into their mouths. I am convinced that such a natural and necessary self-purification of society will only strengthen our country."

The 'I', we decide, is pointedly referring to Vladimir Putin. It is the biggest bulk threat he can make to the people around the table. I wonder who else has received it.

Vitalievich looks around the table to his various oligarchs. It is obvious that they will fold. They can't play this superheated game with Putin, even if it is mostly a poker player's bluff.

One by one they stand, and their corresponding incoming security groups follow.

I sense that Mr Putin is weaker than he looks, but that makes him dangerous. He plays a grandiose game and is used to winning. His previous Ukrainian adventures came when the Russian economy was in trouble and his polls needed a boost. He has had to spend bandwidth on deterring this plot for a coup but seems to have crushed it with a few well-placed text messages.

I can see Christina scanning the room, looking for anyone who could break rank or attempt anything. I sense that she, Charlie, and I have all worked out that Putin knew about this meeting all along and planted Tsarsko Adam Borisovich to attempt to kill the ringleader. Word of his failure has already got back to the Kremlin which tells us that there must be at least one more Putin supporter in the room.

Vitalievich has worked it out as well. "Go," he says, "Go back to your dachas; we cannot speak of this again." He is broken and now a dead man walking. I wonder if he will see the dawn.

Today, Putin's personal polls continue to slide and barely a quarter of Russians support his party. The protests against the opposition's leader Mr Navalny and his arrest in January were the largest in a decade.

Eventhe situation in Ukraine's neighbour Belarus worry Mr Putin: President Lukashenko has been so weakened by protests that he now depends on Russian support to stay in power. If something similar were to happen to Mr Putin, he has no one to turn to. Facing protests at home, he may lash out abroad, in Ukraine, Belarus or elsewhere.

My headset crackles, Antanov speaks, "Visitors, Spetznaz, twelve, incoming."

Christina hears the message too, "Exit, Exit fast. To the pickup point, you too Antonov - bring the Bumerang," she says, picking up her weapon and leaving.

Antanov's voice is heard in the headset, "Copy that, engines are running."

Antanov has done well. The Spetznaz truck is still on the approach road to Vitalievich's property and Antanov's Bumerang APC is already in position.

We climb aboard, Christina and Charlie first, then me. Chantal is in the front cabin with Antanov. Christina swaps places with Chantal. I realise it is so Christina has access to the 30 mm 2A42 automatic guns and the adjacent controls for the Kornet anti-tank guided missiles. I hope we won't need them to clear the area.

Antanov sets a course, which ignores the road and ploughs directly through the fences separating this property from the next one. We can see the Spetznaz carrier arriving at the entrance just as we are making our escape. There are dull thuds and I realise that the incoming troops are using stun grenades, aimed toward the main building complex. Then I hear a receding rattle of sub-machine guns. I'm wondering whether there will be any survivors. Antanov has found a road by now and we bounce on to it. I'm surprised at how fast this monster truck can run and we are soon in open countryside.

"I don't suppose you left that helicopter anywhere useful?" asked Christina.

Antanov smiles, "Funny you should ask that, I dropped it off at Citicopter, which is just around 10 kilometres west, on the E22. We can be there is about 15 minutes."

I notice that Christina is giving Antanov instructions from her cellphone as we navigate through an equestrian centre, which is mysteriously decked out with a range of heavy artillery. Then we are at the Heli Club and Antanov gestures towards his helicopter, neatly stowed outside one of the hangers. We climb out of the back of the Bumerang and as I look back at our transport for the first time, I realise we have been travelling in a camouflaged armoured vehicle with a serious gun mounted forward. What was effectively a major tank.

Now, we walk peacefully across a daisy-strewn field toward the helicopter. Antanov and Christina have hurried ahead and are already starting it up.

The rest of us climb aboard. I wonder where we will be going next.

PART TWO

Never catch me now

On the lam from the law, on the steps of the capitol
You shot a plain clothes cop
On the ten o'clock and I saw momentarily
They flashed a photograph; it couldn't be you

You'd been abused so horribly
But you were there in some anonymous room
And I recall that fall, I was working for the government

And in a bathroom stall off the National Mall
How we kissed so sweetly
How could I refuse a favour or two?
And for a tryst in the greenery
I gave you documents and microfilm too

It was late one night, I was awoken by the telephone
I heard a strangled cry on the end of the line
Purloined in Petrograd, they were suspicious
Of where your loyalties lay,
So, I paid off a bureaucrat
To convince your captors, they're to secret you away

And at the gate of the embassy
Our hands met through the bars
As your whisper stilled my heart
No, they'll never catch me now
No, they'll never catch me
No, they cannot catch me now
We will escape somehow, somehow

It was ten years on
When you resurfaced in a motorcar
And with the wave of an arm
You were there and gone

Colin Meloy

Putin's (alleged) Palace

Now we are again in the air, Christina and Charlie are talking on the headset. They say we will need to visit Putin's Palace.

Antanov wants to fly right out of Russia and to land in Cyprus. He explains he and Cristina 'know some people there.'

Meanwhile, it becomes increasingly obvious to me that Charlie and Christina are planning an assault on Putin's Palace. They are asking Chantal if she is prepared to use some of Limantour's powers. Limantour, the Mistress of Chaos. I worry that we are getting into this situation very deep, but with only a sketchy plan.

To top it all, the Russian President is on record as denying owning the palace, although he is probably using more of his Saint Petersburg tactics of concealment. I wonder if we will get into somewhere that is the wrong place.

I check the internet from my phone. The current owner of the Palace is shown as Arkady Romanovich Rotenberg, a Russian billionaire businessman and oligarch. With his brother Boris Rotenberg, he was co-owner of the Stroygazmontazh (S.G.M. group), the largest construction company for gas pipelines and electrical power supply lines in Russia. He is a close confidant, business partner, and childhood friend of Putin. With an estimated fortune at $2.5 billion, Rotenberg became a billionaire through lucrative state-sponsored construction projects and oil pipelines. He has been implicated through the Pandora Papers leak in facilitating and maintaining elaborate networks of offshore wealth for Russian political and economic elites.

A video called 'Putin's Palace' was released by Mr Alexei Anatolievich Navalny, the leader of the Russian Opposition party. His investigation alleges the property cost £1bn ($1.37bn) and was paid for "with the largest bribe in history".

The palace, by the Black Sea, was allegedly financed by billionaires close to Mr Putin. It is said to have a casino, skating rink and vineyard.

"They built a palace for their boss with this money," Mr Navalny says in the video.

For years Navalny has castigated Mr Putin's administration on social media, accusing the Russian leader of feudal patronage and running a system riddled with thieves.

The video also alleges that Russia's Federal Security Service (FSB) owns some 27 square miles (70 square kilometres) of land around the palace, near the resort of Gelendzhik.

Navalny, Russia's most prominent opposition leader, is locked in jail by Putin. Navalny was the survivor of a near-fatal nerve agent attack, escaped Russia but was arrested upon his return to Moscow from Berlin.

Mr Putin called the palace video a 'compilation and montage' and said he found it 'boring'.

'Nothing that is listed there as my property belongs to me or my close relatives, and never did,' he said.

'No one should seek to advance their ambitious objectives and goals, particularly in politics, through protests,' President Putin said, in an apparent reference to Mr Navalny.

In 2017 Mr Navalny's Anti-Corruption Foundation (FBK) also accused ex-Prime Minister Dmitry Medvedev - one of Mr Putin's closest associates - of collecting luxury estates through a secret fortune. Mr Medvedev denied the allegations, dismissing them as 'nonsense'.

Antanov is landing the Kamov-62.

"Welcome to Kursk," he says, "We are around 550 kilometres from Leshkovo. I think we should trade up this helicopter now." He gestures to a white plane standing outside of a hanger. My first thought of its appearance is 'menacing'.

"We'll be using this plane for the next leg. I expect by now they have organised to look for the Kamov. But I don't think they'll be expecting us in a strategic bomber. Let's climb into the Tupolev Tu-160M2. Notice how it has the reflective paint to deflect nuclear blasts. We can fly this as fast as a fighter jet and at a good height. Sorry, but there's only four proper seats, someone will have to ride on the jump."

"How are we getting this into Cyprus?" asks Chantal. "I mean it is somewhat noticeable, and I don't want us to get shot down. A Russian jet in Cypriot airspace?"

"Taken care of," answers Christina, "We've called up Blackbird and he has arranged diplomatic clearance. It's obvious that he is rooting for us, although I fear his days in the Secret Service may be numbered."

Antanov checked around the plane. I realised he was looking at the on-board weaponry. "We've picked up this plane, which seems to be carrying 4 AS-15 missiles, but nothing else. The AS-15 or Kh-55 is an air-launched cruise missile developed by the Soviet Union. They can deliver a 250 Kilo-ton nuclear warhead 2,500 km. So, we'd better be careful how we fly this thing."

We climb aboard and I uprate my review of the plane from 'menacing' to 'lethal' as I look back into the weapons hold and see missiles hanging in their release apparatus.

"250 Kt is about 5 times the power of the bombs detonated in World War II, and this plane is carrying 4 of them. It has capacity to carry 16. That's enough to wipe out the entire eastern seaboard of the USA," observes Charlie, "We are flying World War III".

"Scrive, you can fly planes?" asks Antonov, "How would you like to be flight engineer on this one?" He points me to a seat and panel of dials and controls, and I realise that the 'glass cockpit' design still has some traditional controls further back for each of the engines. Christina quickly shows me around the controls and even fires up a couple of the engines. I realise she knows her stuff about big planes too.

Antanov is readying for take-off and has Christina seated

as co-pilot again. She appears to be concentrating in a way I've not seen before.

Then we taxi to the end of the military runaway and I notice several ground staff stop what they are doing and come over to watch the take-off.

I think I'm prepared, but this plane is built to a military specification and has four after-burning turbofan engines, to blast it along the runway. Christina and Antanov seen unperturbed as they pull this killing machine into the air. I feel the screech from the four jets as we climb to our cruising altitude. I just hope we won't get shot down.

In around an hour we are over Cyprus mercifully escorted in by two NATO F-35A fighter planes. I'm getting used to this drill now, but it is reassuring to have Antanov in the pilot's seat, who has been in similar situations. I find it fascinating that so much of the so-called air superiority is in planes that were designed 10 or 20 years ago. The F-35 is already 15 years old and the Tu-160 jet plane we are riding is around 35 years old.

We land and the same thing happens with ground crew here in RAF Akrotiri, where many people come out to look at this sleek, menacing white plane bearing Russian insignia. We are clearly a rare spectacle even among the hardened aircrews stationed at this base.

I look at Antanov and can see he is relieved to be back on the ground. He's had a tough day, with stakeouts, shootouts, driving a tank, a helicopter, and a jet bomber to bring us all to this island in the middle of the Mediterranean.

But I sense that Charlie and Christina are tightening the

screws even further.

Cyprus - Artem and Dakis

I'm acutely aware that we are still travelling on Dutch passports, with glued-in Russian visas.

Christina says something to the base security and we are all admitted without any further questions.

"I was here during one of the terrorism troubles and know the woman who is now the base Commander," explains Christina, "I've asked to meet her at some point while we are here."

"Well, we should hit the town tonight, to discuss our next moves," says Chantal, "I can already sense that Charlie has a plan, maybe with Christina too."

"Yes, and don't be surprised if you are roped into it too," says Charlie, "And you, Scrive!" She looks at me and I know this will be something wild.

Although a military base, RAF Akrotiri has the trappings of a small commercial airport, with a coffee shop, lounge area and for us, on this occasion, the all-important cab rank.

We take a large taxi, which is like minibus, and Christina asks for Limassol centre. We are on the hunt for somewhere to relax. The taxi driver, who introduces himself as Artem, suggests the Dionysus Mansion and we all agree to go there. He says that his brother Dakis is a waiter there, and that the food is very good.

He drives us out of the base and then turns east along the coast, before heading slightly inland to what I imagine is the centre of Limassol. At least, it is where the post office is situated. Then, he takes us to the restaurant, the last few metres on foot, and introduces us to his brother.

Call me a cynic, but I'm used to taxi drivers having that kind of line to get extra commission from the tavernas, but this seemed genuine. His brother shows us to a beautiful corner table, outside in a small sun bathed square and shaded by a large olive tree. Perfect. I can feel the tension drain away. I can see the same effect in the others too.

We order food in what is now the customary way, a selection that we can place in the middle of the table and then select our own, buffet style. Dakis brings us some Maratheftiko red wine and pours us each a glass.

"The first is on the house," he says, "You all look as if you need some good hospitality. After the first bottle you will all start to experience the magic of Cyprus."

Late afternoon turns into evening as we sit around this table. I notice, still that the sky has turned a green colour, before it darkens and I wonder if there has been some pollution of which I am unaware.

"I'm troubled that I can't remember this time," I say, "When I try to think about what happens, all I can remember is the Klima Wars, but I can't remember how they start, let alone anything about Putin."

"Me also," says Charlie, "It is so unusual for us, as Watchers to not have any sense of recall of this time."

Chantal speaks, "I've been wondering that too. I wonder if we have somehow been dropped into a Variation. Remember that stuff about when the world was supposed to be flat, or the scientists thought that the sun orbited the Earth.

"As Watchers we all say that the cosmic dealer smiles within his darkened room. He doesn't let on that there are other darkened rooms next door. You just must think of them."

She smiles cheekily, "It's a principle of my Chaos, as Limantour."

Then she continues, "Other darkened rooms can contain different frames of reference. In the Lepton Epoch he may have stumbled upon Light and his form of physics, but only in one of the frames of reference."

"At least one of these dark areas of deep shadow contains a key to explain what is happening.

"Think of parallel universes.

"We all know that the wrinkle in human thinking is that although multiple metaverses exist, it is not possible to travel between them. But maybe, just maybe, we have."

I understand Limantour's thought spoken by Chantal. It explains the small variances we are experiencing. The green sky, the larger-than-they-should-be cats and dogs.

The sudden, pervasive use of electric road vehicles. Chantel's theory could explain why we can't remember. If we are in a parallel metaverse, then we won't have experienced it before.

Charlie nods, "I think you could be right, Chantal, but this world is so detailed and torn with the same anguish as the one we left."

"I assume it is an effect from the Trigax, which fired us all back to this point. I can't understand how it would have the precision to bring us all to the same point unless it was somehow significant. Something controlled."

I remember something from a long time ago, before I became Scrive and when I was a Watcher. I'd been in a Chinese wet fish market with Lepton and Lekton. Lepton was a projection of Light and Lekton was a projection of Darkness, teaming up with Scheppach to create ever-increasing vestiges of warfare.

Scheppach the illegal arms dealer - a Bladerunner - provided her escalating devices of warfare, which began with knives, then guns and continued to increase in magnitude.

"Could it be that something has happened between Lepton and Lekton? " I ask.

Chantal looks concerned, "Yes, I can almost sense it. I wondered why my normal Limantour chaos moves were not available. Everything I must call on is now distressing instead of playful. It makes sense if we are in a different reality."

Christina and Antanov look on puzzled whilst we have this conversation.

"Look, have you had some magic mushrooms, or maybe the wine is too strong?" suggests Antanov.

Christina speaks, "No, Antanov, I think these people really have a gift. Remember, in our Russian culture: *nechistaya magiya* - unclean magic, and *produktivnaya magiya* - good, productive magic. Most productive magic was homeopathic, meaning that a symbolic action was performed with the hope of evoking a related response from reality.

Antanov agrees, "Yes, I remember that children's springtime ritual of carrying around branches with artificial birds or cookies. It was thought to help bring about the bird flight associated with the coming of spring."

This is all getting multi-layered.

I wonder if we need to do a symbolic act to evoke a response from our original reality.

That we have been flipped by the Trigax railgun into a historical instance that seems real but is one step removed from the Earth that we all know.

Maybe we have somehow slipped from Lepton's world filled with Light into an adjacent one of Darkness? Lekton and Scheppach's dark room.

Too much paperwork

We finish the meal, but the last discussion had thrown us all off kilter. We still don't have plan, other than to stay somewhere overnight.

Dakis calls his brother who arrives with the taxi-bus and takes as all to a spectacular apartment complex.

"It's my cousin," Artem explains, "She owns the whole complex here, I'm sure you will get a deal. Here, let me talk to them."

He dials a number and speaks quickly in a Greek dialect to someone. We'd all been speaking in English and I don't think he realised that three of us could also follow his conversation in Greek.

True to his word, he arranges for us to have a floor of apartments, and then he explains to us that it was considered 'off-season' by the owner. He had therefore obtained them for us at a special rate. We would need to go to the reception, but to say that Artem had sent some 'special guests'.

"You know something," said Christina, "I think we

should stay here for a couple of days. Recharge and get off the radar of Putin and Vitalievich.

"Won't they miss the long-range strategic bomber?" asks Charlie.

"Relax," says Antanov, "Blackbird and I have settled it with the right people. They think the stealth bomber is secretly in the air somewhere, and the Brits on the base won't be declaring they have it."

'Too much paperwork,' I surmise.

We check in and take the elevator to our floor. We have five modern and well-appointed bedrooms spread across three studio suites. The views are breath-taking and look out across the Mediterranean. We have balconies with sofas and can sit in the evening air.

I settle into my room and switch on the television. Unlike in Russia, we once again have news feeds which describe the war in the Ukraine. Now it has moved on to allegations of biological and chemical warfare.

A Russian foreign ministry spokesperson is accusing Ukraine of developing biological weapons with the assistance of the United States.

The US vehemently denies these claims, arguing that it is Russia who wants to use these weapons of mass destruction.

I muse that it is a classic use of misinformation to normalise a potentially aggressive move. The US Press Secretary is publishing tweets (diplomacy gone mad?) stating that Russia is using these allegations as propaganda in a bid to pave the way for its own use of biological and chemical arms.

In Chantel's words, "This Version of the world is even crazier that the one where we have been Watchers."

I think that it would not be the first time that Russia has accused another state of poisonous warfare as a means of justifying these weapons' use, either by itself or an ally.

I remember that when President Bashar al-Assad used chemical weapons in Syria, Vladimir Putin backed up the allegation that it was rebels who had used them in attacks.

US officials described this as a classic Soviet trick: accuse the enemy of what you want to do yourself to legitimise your later actions.

I have a hazy recollection of something, some kind of vaccine permanently triggered and connected to the arm by a small cartridge. Tropus? Something like that. Something to counteract the effects of nerve agents and lethal viruses. I realise it is something that must happen in the future and it dawns on me that it must be a consequence of the Klima Wars. I check with Charlie and she has a similar recollection.

But would Putin use these contentious and highly destructive weapons? If so, Scheppach the arms dealer would have her work cut out.

Putin is already said to have employed other extremely controversial weapons, such as thermobaric weapons (also known as a vacuum bombs) and cluster bombs.

These attacks have not been limited to military targets such as weapon stockpiles but have also been used against civilians. Attacks have been recorded against civilian targets such as hospitals and a maternity ward. There are also reports that Putin has now used a chemical weapon: white phosphorus.

Putin considers chemical weapons effective at breaking down enemy defences. Assad used chemical arms in Syria for precisely this reason. Chemicals were deployed against rebel defences when conventional bombings had not been sufficient to overcome them – for example, at Douma near Damascus.

If Putin has employed white phosphorous in Ukraine, it would be no surprise if he escalated to using other forms of chemical, such as nerve agents. Russia has, in the past experimented with every type of weapon. Choking agents like phosgene attack the lungs and respiratory system, causing the victim to drown in their lungs' secretions. There are blister agents, like mustard gas, which burns the skin and blinds people.

And then there is the most lethal category of all: nerve agents, which interfere with the brain's messages to the body's muscles. A tiny drop of these can be fatal. Less than 0.5mg of VX nerve agent, for example, is enough to kill an adult.

All these so-called chemical agents can be used in warfare in artillery shells, bombs, and missiles. They can even be sprayed from the sky. But all are strictly prohibited by the Chemical Weapons Convention of 1997, signed by most nations, including Russia.

Russia says it destroyed the last of its chemical weapons stocks in 2017 but since then there have been at least two chemical attacks blamed on Moscow.

The first was the Salisbury attack of March 2018 when a former KGB officer and defector, Sergei Skripal, was poisoned along with his daughter by the nerve agent Novichok. Russia denied responsibility and came up with over 20 different explanations for who could have done it.

But investigators concluded it was the work of two officers from Russia's GRU military intelligence and as a result 128 Russian spies and diplomats were expelled from several countries. Then, in August 2020, the prominent Russian opposition activist Alexei Navalny was also poisoned with Novichok and narrowly escaped death.

Later, during the Ukrainian war, a sanctioned Russian oligarch Roman Abramovich reportedly suffered from symptoms of poisoning after meeting with Russian and Ukrainian representatives and attempting to broker peace negotiations between the two countries. Abramovich allegedly suffered from a temporary loss of eyesight, problems eating, and peeling skin on his face and hands after a meeting with Ukrainian and Russian representatives in Kyiv. He said he'd only drunk water and eaten chocolate at the meetings.

These were similar symptoms to those suffered by Ukrainian President Viktor Yushchenko when an attempt to assassinate him failed during the Ukrainian elections. Yushchenko was confirmed to have ingested tetra-chloro-dibenzo-dioxin (TCDD), the most potent dioxin and contaminant in Agent Orange

If Russia were to use weapons like poison gas in its war, this would be seen as crossing a major red line, most probably prompting calls for the West to take decisive action.

The problem is there is a potentially a grey area between working on ways to protect your population from harmful pathogens, and secretly working on how they could be used as a weapon. Russia did not produce any immediate evidence of Ukrainian misdoings in this area. But it called for an emergency UN Security Council meeting on Friday to discuss its claims.

Russia, when it was part of the Soviet Union, controlled a truly massive biological weapons programme, run by an agency called Biopreparat. that employed about 70,000 people.

After the end of the Cold War, scientists went in to dismantle the Soviet Union's massive biological weapons programme, run by an agency called Biopreparat. They found the Soviets had mass produced and weaponised anthrax, smallpox, and other diseases after testing them on live monkeys on an island in southern Russia. They had even loaded anthrax spores into the warheads of long-range inter-continental missiles aimed at Western cities.

Finally, in this grim roll call of non-conventional weapons, there is the "dirty bomb" - a normal explosive that is surrounded by radioactive elements. It is known as an RDD - a radiological dispersal device. It could be a conventional explosive carrying a radioactive isotope such as Caesium 60 or Strontium 90.

It wouldn't necessarily kill any more people than a normal bomb, initially at least. But it could render a huge area uninhabitable for weeks, until it had been fully decontaminated.

A dirty bomb is almost like a psychological weapon,

designed to cause panic among a population and undermine the morale of a society.

The attacks on single people took place after the claim that Russia had disarmed – although Russia denies that it was involved in these assaults. However, on that basis, we can assume that Putin has access to chemical stockpiles which could be deployed in Ukraine.

I think back to what Dr Gvasalia briefed, "Putin accepts, like some psychopaths, that if they are going to lose, so must everyone else. Putin will want to preserve the way he believes Russia should be.

No wonder Vitalievich wanted to stop Putin. If Putin is playing a psychopathic endgame, it will hurt everyone.

Dr Gvasalia had speculated that Putin must realise there is going to come a time when he is going to have to hand over the reins.

But this creates contradictions. Putin wanting to bring back old Russia, even with many around him against this. Some that he trusts - even from his boyhood - are now in their seventies and may not be useful to his cause for much longer. He has created a citizenship living under his misinformation believing one thing which is becoming increasingly difficult to manipulate.

No wonder he is rummaging in the back of his weapons locker.

I wonder how I can recall this information with such clarity, yet don't know about the start of the Klima Wars.

I also remember that biological weapons are more difficult than chemical arms because biological agents are contagious. Contagion means that if an aggressor uses a biological weapon, there is every chance that their own troops will catch the disease they have released. This "boomerang effect" may deter Putin.

However, the Vector laboratory in Koltsovo (near Novosibirsk)—formerly part of the Biopreparat complex—intends to continue its research on pox viruses and is very dangerous because of possible changes in the Russian government.

When General Lebed was asked about the nuclear and biological capability of Russia, he replied that because the Russian Army is very weak, Russia still needs these weapons to protect itself.

Imagine the situation in a mountainous region like Chechnya or Afghanistan. It's very difficult to fight in the mountains using conventional weapons. But a single plane or cruise missile armed with biological weapons could kill absolutely everybody in any deep valley in the mountains. So, the Russians consider these weapons highly effective for certain types of conflict.

I think again of the cornered rat that Putin so frequently references.

Plans

We all go to meet in Christina's room. She has the best suite, we decide, with a long sofa set up on the balcony overlooking the sea. They have designed Limassol with a dual carriageway along the seafront and most of the buildings, including ours, set back maybe 50 metres. It's a similar setup to the South of France - maybe Cannes - but not as elegant.

Christina, Charlie and Antanov are engrossed in a conversation. I can see they are plotting our next moves.

Chantal walks in and when we are all seated, Charlie summarises.

"We've got several assets. A long-range Russian stealth bomber with four nuclear cruise missiles. We know where Putin's Palace is and we are within comfortable flying distance. Even from here, one of the cruise missiles could make its way to Krasnodar Krai without interruption. The problem is with the 250 Kiloton nuclear warheads, it's not as if we can dial them back a little.

"Set to stun?" says Chantal.

Charlie continues, "Antanov also reminds us that at the eastern end of Cyprus we have access to drones. They are Turkish Bayraktar UAVs, based at Geçitkale Air Base from where they are tested."

Antanov interrupts: "They are Bayraktar TB2 combat tactical unmanned aerial vehicle systems and are already being used by Ukraine, from Ukrainian soil, to target Russian tank convoys. They can carry Roketsan's MAM (Smart Micro Munition)'s and TUBITAK-SAGE BOZOK laser-guided bombs."

"But how would we get to the weapons?" asked Christina, "The stealth bomber we stole, so it can be re-used, but the drones are under Turkish control. The Turkish are on the fence about this war now, because of the direct threat to their own country."

Charlie continues, "So we have access to weaponry, but some of it is too powerful and the rest is inaccessible and probably too lightweight."

Antanov continues, still intent on developing his hybrid plan.

"Often during heightened conflicts, it is hard to distinguish between factual events and misinformation - like the way some videos of drone attacks have already been exposed as fakes. Given the chaotic events on the ground, it is almost impossible to assess how often and how successfully Ukraine has utilised its Turkish drones so far. We do know that Ukraine bought Bayraktar-TB2 over the past years and that Turkey and Ukraine signed an agreement for the production within Ukrainian borders of the TB2."

"Now, sitting right here in Cyprus, is a major flight

base for these Bayraktar drones. And ever since 2019, Kyiv has bought dozens of these drones from Ankara."

"We could create a haze of confusion by sending a whole squadron of these things across to Russia. Purely as a diversion

"Then, it will depend on Russian air defences. Drones like the TB2 are vulnerable to anti-air defence systems. To be effective, they need to be employed in a savvy way, in coordination with other electronic warfare systems that 'blind' enemy radars and through appropriate tactics. However, we know that Russian Air-superiority is suspect. They may have planes, but how many of them are functional?

"In Libya, Russian forces figured out effective ways to counter Turkish tactics and shoot down their drones. The same has been observed in Syria and Nagorno-Karabakh,

"Nonetheless, the fact that Ukraine could strike Russian ground forces with TB2 suggests either that Russian forces are advancing without air defence – which is very well possible, considering the logistical and organisational problems Russia has encountered so far.

Charlie shakes her head, "But we've no control over the drones. The Turks are hardly likely to do what we say."

"Looking like this, I agree," says Chantal, "But what about if we changed our appearance?" she walks out of the room with Charlie and a few moments later returns in the clothing of a Turkish Tümgeneral. Two star plus crossed swords epaulette insignia and a blue beret.

"Wow," says Christina, "That is some transformation.

You are suddenly a hot high-ranking Turkish NATO officer."

"The very model of a modern major general!" says Antanov.

We all laugh.

Charlie continues, "So, with Chantal's revised identity, we can probably influence the way that the drones get used. Also, either approach - the bomber or the drones - will look deliberate and can set off further chain reactions. We think that Vitalievich's plan to the oligarchs was to get closer to Putin and then to act. Putin seems to deploy poison against his enemies and that could be a better way to stop him."

Antanov grimaces, "But poisoning or similar is rather more 'hands on' than either of the other approaches, both of which can be run from a safe distance."

Charlie adds, "Yes, but that's where our other asset comes in. Three assets. Three of us are Watchers and would get bounced back on the time-line."

Chantal adds, "I've been thinking and it may also be a way to break us out of this alternative world-view, back onto our original one, even with all of its faults. Where skies are blue and cats are small enough to look cute on the internet."

"So how many of us can you shapeshift like this?" asks Antanov.

"I expect I can do you all, but only one at a time," says Charlie, "It uses considerable energy. And now I need to turn Chantal back into her own clothes."

Hey remember (mashup)

Hey, remember that time when I would only read
Shakespeare
Hey, remember that other time when I would only read
the backs of cereal boxes
Hey, remember that time when my favourite colours
was pink and green
Hey, remember that month when I only ate boxes of Tangerines,
so cheap and juicy

Tangerines

Hey, remember that time when I would only smoke Parliaments
Hey, remember that time when I would only smoke Marlboros
Hey, remember that time when I would only smoke Camels
Hey, remember that time when I was broke
I didn't care I just borrowed from my friends

Bum bum bum bum bum
Bum bum bum bum bum

Regina Spektor, adapted

Remember that time (Lepton reprise)

I looked towards Chantal.

"You remember that time?" I asked, "When we were Watchers and you summoned up Lepton and Lekton?" It was just before we ran our Intervention that saved Earth?"

"Oh yes, " said Chantal, "As Limantour, I was able to bring about all manner of chaotic events. Like that dingy Huanan apartment over the wet market. Although the unintended consequence was a global pandemic."

At that time, we, as Watchers, had been flipped to Southern China, when suddenly Lepton and a stranger - who I discovered was Lekton - had appeared.

Lepton had beamed when he saw me. "Hello, Farallon, it has been a long time! You asked to see me and to witness for yourself that I have continued to enjoy a good living beyond your metaverse."

Metaverse. That was the key word. He was referring to us being in one frame of reference, but that there could be others.

I could see what Lepton had done. Lepton was the originator of one of the earliest Interventions - the provision of Light for the universe. The Lepton Epoch.

Lekton was almost Lepton's opposite. Watchers knew that Lekton's intervention was to bring warfare to humanity. I had stood with the bringers of Light and Darkness.

Lekton had gone on to explain that we were in the workshop of Scheppach. She lived outside laws and created necessary evil in the form of ever-escalating methods of warfare.

When we were contemplating the first Intervention, Lekton had explained, "You should see now that whatever happens, you get placed in our metaverse after your Intervention. I'm sure you have seen that for Darnell, Bishop, Cardinal, Abbott, Lepton, and myself, it becomes a rewarding journey."

Then I remembered Scheppach's words: "We are seeing a shift now. Earth was able to keep itself balanced through increasingly vicious warfare. Now we are seeing a mixed effect. Part of it is through warfare, but this has been hybridised by the onslaught of other methods, such as the biological. The potential for 230 million cases of COVID and around five million worldwide deaths from the disease. Like the 25 million from Spanish flu."

Scheppach had gestured to some small canisters stood along a shelf. I realised they were various toxins.

Lekton spoke, "Earth rebalances, seeking a new equilibrium." I remembered Lekton was stuttering, like a poor-quality video, when I realised, I had run out of time with him.

Chantal spoke as if she was recounting Limantour's experience, "We left that place around when things started to stutter and become unstable. I think if we had been able to stay longer, we would have discovered more."

Christina and Antanov were looking towards us with their earlier suspension of disbelief.

Christina asked, "So what was in the canisters?"

And Antanov, "Did Scheppach start the COVID pandemic?"

Chantal answered, "Remember I, as Limantour am Mistress of Chaos. It means that sometimes things that don't happen seem very real, although I don't think this whole reality is a projection."

"Can you remember how to summon Lepton?" I ask.

"Oh yes but be careful what you wish for. In this metaverse some things are already different. I would not want Lepton to be totally changed."

"It's mainly our sense of the future that is missing," I said.

There was a shudder like a small earthquake. I noticed, from the balcony, a few larger than average waves on the sea. Waves that were moving against the tide and away from the shoreline.

I looked around the room, and an extra person was sitting amidst our group. It was Lepton.

"I am glad you called, Limantour!" he said, "Hello everyone, Farallon, Limantour, Tomales!" I could see that Lepton was already flickering slightly, like he was having trouble holding on to this reference frequency.

"You were right. This is an alternative metaverse. It is very close to the one you are accustomed to. After you left the fish market, a couple of further things happened. Lekton was already hostile and wanted revenge. He decided to try to reframe the worldview, using Putin as a human blunt instrument. Like a cheap movie with an arch villain, only played for real. Scheppach helped him, with the idea of increasing her arsenal."

"How do we get to Lekton?"

"He's gone. He finally met his end in the future, but within a few hundred years of now. He never visited this exact time and can't shed a direct influence upon it."

"What did Lekton do?

"He manipulated Putin, who was already a deeply troubled human."

"Then he called the four of you across to this world. He called for four of you and achieved three."

"And Scheppach?"

"She picked from the row of canisters. Selected COVID and let it run its course."

"But if we hadn't Intervened?"

"None of this would have happened. Remember unintended consequences."

Lepton continues, "I tried to put a marker in this metaverse, to keep people away and to make things difficult for Lekton. I modified my version of Lepton's atomic model and removed the tau and tau neutrino from the set of elementary particles. It was enough to mark this world as unstable. The green skies, the large pets, the early adoption of electric automobiles. Without the tau, the Chaos Frame will gently collapse."

"What? You condemned this reality?"

"Remember it is only a facsimile of the world view you have viewed for all of time. This copy is broken, thanks to Lekton and Scheppach.

"You can afford to do anything here; you will be bounced back into your own worldview at the end. You are fortunate, Drake is keeping your place in the other reality. Drake, now called Nathan, was outside the influence of the Trigax guns fired by Lekton. Nathan lives in in Bodø, Norway, with his partner Sheri. It is fortunate he lives within the Arctic Circle and the Trigax rail guns are orbiting the equator. He is out of their range."

We all look as Lepton's image sputtered and then disappeared.

Chantal speaks, "Don't worry, he's fine, it is just difficult to hold him in another reality view for more than a few minutes."

She walks across the balcony, and as she does so, her polka dot dress changes colour. The dots change from pink to blue.

"Sorry," she says, "Bringing Lepton here has drained me."

Charlie's Plan

Charlie speaks, "Seeing Lepton was incredibly helpful. Now we know that this variation, this metaverse, is a step away from the one we have watched."

Chantal nods, "The ancient Greek word 'chaos' means a chasm or void, and its opposite is 'cosmos', meaning the exquisite design of the world. We've been flipped from the cosmic into the chaotic. But hold that thought. We need some food. Or another way, I need some food after that draining Lepton experience."

Christina flipped her phone, "Here: Bolt. It's like Deliveroo or Doordash in many places. The Cypriot equivalent."

We all leaned over her phone, which displayed screen after screen of burger joints, with imaginative names like The B.B. King and The Big Cheese.

"Is that all they do?" asks Antanov.

"There's the Wings of Love, which is chicken wings, and Pizza Paradise," answered Christina.

In the end we decided we'd go for Most Popular Choices which was burgers and so we ordered five burgers, fries, Tasty Onion Rings, plus Cokes. It would be difficult for that to be a total failure. The burgers looked like they were well stacked with salads too. 20-25 minutes, it explained.

I remember that astrophysicists are struck by what they call the "fine-tuning" of the universe, a place which looks as though it saw us coming and framed its laws accordingly.

It's why Lepton has influenced this variant but held back some the components. The third order fermions. The tau leptons. It's an elegant form of sabotage. Maybe the pervasive burger joints are another sign. To bring a system to a gentle collapse.

I ask, "But what about Christina and Antanov? If all of this collapses we Watchers just get flipped to another position on the timeline. Christina and Antanov are humans."

Chantal nods, "But don't you see? One minute they are in the normal Earth metaverse. The one we watched for so long. Then, they manifest in this alternative. If it ends, they will find themselves back in their normal existence, at the point where they left. Except they will have some serious enlightenment! I've seen this before."

She continues, "Trust me, as Limantour, the Mistress of Chaos, I have seen other universes a lot more chaotic than our own. Chaos Theory deals with systems whose behaviour is random and unpredictable. One could even think of Vladimir Putin as such a system.

Antanov adds, "One curious feature of the Russian

president's attack on Ukraine is its recklessness. Former KGB agents may be callous, thick-headed or sadistic, but one would not expect them to be impetuous."

I can't help thinking that Putin was a ruthless KGB man a long time ago and has had plenty of time to go mad and be surrounded by sycophants. His motive in flattening Ukraine is partly ethnic. He thinks that the country is a fiction, a cardboard cut-out nation, and should be wound up as soon as possible. He sees Ukraine as a void, a non-entity, and Russia will impose some order on this chaos by incorporating it into itself, making him a mini-tsar.

Chantal adds, "I've walked on the rough ground of what Ludwig Wittgenstein called social existence, even if there are those who try to walk on the pure ice of some flawless vision of order.

"But I see the catch. The two are not simply opposites. Now I see in Ukraine how easily such flawless visions create the rough ground of a city brought to ruin."

The Czarlings

The entry phone rings. It's a guy with the food. We ask him to bring it up to our floor. Then there is due ceremony as it is handed out. The guy has brought some 'optional' cold beers too. He sells them to us in a separate deal. Genius.

Charlie speaks, "The oligarchs know that Russia is far less important than China, either to the world economy or to climate talks. But it still matters a great deal.

"These oligarchs, like the ones assembled by Vitalievich, also know that Russia, because of Putin, is the single most prolific stoker of instability on Europe's borders. The Kremlin has become the most energetic troublemaker in rich democracies, funding extremist parties, spreading disinformation, discord and eroding these oligarchs' wealth.

She continues, "Now, it becomes a question of how the West deals with Putin. It will set a precedent. China's leaders are certainly watching, even as they straddle both relationships. If the world lets Russia roll over Ukraine, the Chinese may assume that Taiwan is fair game, too."

I think it is one way that the Klima Wars could start. I wish I could remember. I wish any of us Watchers could remember.

Antanov speaks, "We can consider a hybrid attack on Putin. Blend together our assets and run some confusion. By the sound of it, Chantal will be good at assisting that?"

Chantal lets out a squee of delight and jumps up. I notice she has suddenly changed into new clothes. Earthy colours, a green, grey, and brown geometrically blocked top, and matching green shorts. Suddenly she has blonde shoulder length hair and I realise she is pulling a full chaos move on us all.

'Sorry," she says, "but that encounter with Lepton took it out of me. I've changed my look to generate some new energy."

Charlie looks at her enviously, "Those clothes..."

"I know, I look like a boy now. I'm calling this look 'boyish femininity!"

I realise that Chantal still has Limantour's full Watcher powers.

Christina continues, "Right, now if we can get to the northeastern end of Cyprus, we can try to gain access to many drone weapons."

Antanov adds, "And we still have the bomber. It's a problem here in Cyprus because the island is divided into so many nation states. The plane is landed in the United Kingdom, we are in Greek Cyprus and the drones are in Turkish Cyprus."

"I know, I could have designed this country," says Chantal, "It's so - multifaceted."

"Well, we need to think about moving that Tu-160 stealth bomber before someone misses it, " says Antanov, "We put it on a 'round the globe' mission, but it would have run out of fuel by now. The paperwork to find it will have started in Russia."

Christina nodded, "And we don't want to lose it as an asset for this campaign."

Charlie asked, "The thing is, Putin could be in any of several places. You know he has gone to ground and is only making pre-recorded TV speeches now. He could be in Moscow, The Kremlin, at one of the dachas or at his Palace."

"Or in the Altai Mountains, in Siberia, in his underground bunker - the one where he has sent his family," says Chantal.

"Ah you know about that?" asks Antanov, "I had to go there once. It isn't a bunker, more like an underground city, equipped with the latest science and technology. It's supposed to be a sprawling mountain resort built by energy company Gazprom around a decade ago in the Ongudaysky district of the Altai Republic, a region of Siberia bordering Mongolia, China and Kazakhstan."

Antanov is looking toward the sea, "I was there, in Altai, with a secure team checking the exit paths. Blackbird requested it. As a simulation, we had to create an incident and attempt to stop the occupants from leaving. They had multiple escape routes; road, a double heliport, even the river, but most of the complex is hidden underground. It is like a hidden city. For us, it was like a version of cat and mouse. Think of a mountain hideout, with luxurious above ground facilities and then enough power to run a small city, most of which is underground. "

Antanov continues, "I'll say this is rumour, but Putin's 'other' wife was there when we were, Alina Kabaeva - some 30 years younger. She is alleged to be the Russian leader's secret spouse - although a Russian newspaper was closed down for reporting it. She's that Olympic Gold-winning rhythmic gymnast, who became a wealthy politician in the Duma and then a high ranking official in the National Media Group. Sometimes you just can't make this stuff up.

Putin's two daughters - The Czarlings - I think their names are Maria and Katerina, are from his previous marriage to former flight attendant Lyudmila Shkrebneva. They are almost the same age as Alina Kabaeva. Putin is alleged to have two sons and twin daughters with Kabaeva.

He looked around, "The Kabaeva family have Swiss passports and are probably in Putin's Swiss chalet.
"Then he has another daughter - Elizaveta from a previous relationship with cleaner-turned-multimillionaire Svetlana Krivonogikh, now a part-owner of a major Russian bank. See how the money rubs off."

Antanov shrugs, "I reckon if Putin has sent them to the chalet, then it is partly for their protection and partly so they can't see what he is doing.

"Defence Minister Shoigu is currently in personal control of Russia's military operation in Ukraine. It was him that arranged for Putin to attend a shamanic ritual in Siberia which involved the sacrifice of a black wolf in a rite to improve the president's health.

"Is that both physical health and mental?" asks Christina.

Antanov says, "According to my sources, which are largely men on the ground, they are saying that Putin was suffering from early-stage Parkinson's disease, and that he has a secret life-threatening illness - maybe throat cancer being treated with steroids, but they have no proof. It ties in with the medication rumours."

Christina answers, "We must see Putin for what he is. A psychopathic killer. But he also keeps communications open, although it is deceitful and only Putin's attempt to boost his prestige. He doesn't want to de-escalate military tensions nor to signal resolution. He just wants to pretend to negotiate to buy time for his hapless and bullied troops to regroup and continue their frightened onslaught.

She continues, "In the end it will not be outsiders who decide Russia's future. The long, hard task of creating an alternative to Mr Putin's misrule can be performed only by Russians themselves. Meanwhile, democracies should lend Russian democrats their moral support, just as they did in the Soviet era. The U.S. President should press hard for Mr Navalny to be released, immediately and unharmed.

Christina continues, "The world needs dissidents like Navalny to hold the Kremlin to account. Without such checks, Russia will remain a thuggish kleptocracy, and its neighbours will never be safe."

Russkiy Mir

Christina explains, "Look I know you won't have as much depth as Antanov and me on Russian matters. We have both been through the training in Russia. I can see it from the inside, as well as later from the outside when we both stepped away from the ideology

Antanov speaks, "Yes, 'Project Russia' is a Russian nonfiction book series written during the first decade of the 21st century. The books have placed highly on bestseller lists in Russia. These books discuss aspects of political, economic, and ideological life in Russia and the world, and try to predict the future.

"Project Russia touched on social questions, saying that Russia faced collapse and needed a unifying idea. State structural problems in Russia were also analysed, exploring the possibility that the Russian Federation might cease to exist.

"The authors of Project Russia predicted the financial crisis of 2007–08 in their 2005 book, describing the approaching unrest and analysing its causes and the fall of the world order."

Christina continues, "Putin's crusade against a liberal European future is being fought in the name of Russkiy mir—'the Russian world', a previously obscure historical term for a Slavic civilisation based on shared ethnicity, religion, and heritage.

The Putin regime has revived, promulgated and debased this idea into an obscurantist anti-Western mixture of Orthodox dogma, nationalism, conspiracy theory and security-state Stalinism."

Antanov adds, "When we used to read the books we were given back in Arkhangelsk, it was noticeable how many were old and skewed in their view of the west. In a hothouse environment this worked, but really it was at odds with reality.

Christina continues, "The war with Ukraine is the latest and most striking manifestation of Putin's revanchist ideological movement. By that I mean Putin's retaliation, to recover what he believes to be lost territory. This time it has brought to the fore a dark and mystical component within it, with Putin a bit in love with death."

It could be a link with Scheppach, I thought.

Eckhart adds, "Putin's first public appearance since the invasion was a rally at the Luzhniki stadium packed with 95,000 flag-waving people, mostly young, some bussed in, many, presumably, there of their own volition.

"And Putin is playing the 'God on their side' card too. An open octagonal structure set up in the middle of the stadium served as an altar. Standing at it Mr Putin praised Russia's army with words from St John's gospel: "Greater love hath no man than this, that a man lay down his life for his friends."

"Putin's oration made much of Fyodor Ushakov, a deeply religious admiral who, in the 18th century, helped win Crimea back from the Ottomans. In 2001 he was canonised by the Orthodox church; he later (and I know this will sound a little crazy) became the patron saint of nuclear-armed long-distance bombers.

"He said that the storms of war would glorify Russia. That is how it was in his time; that is how it is today and will always be!'

Christina adds, "Putin's words and actions were direct from Stalin's playbook. After the Soviet Union was attacked by Germany in 1941, Stalin rehabilitated and co-opted the previously persecuted Orthodox church as a way of rallying the people. He also created a medal for outstanding service by naval officers called the order of Ushakov."

Antanov nods, "Putin's rally is not a mere echo or emulation; there is a strand of history which leads quite directly from then to now. Links between the church and the security forces, first fostered under Stalin then stronger after the fall of Communism.

"The allegiance of its leaders, if not of all its clergy, has now been transferred to Mr Putin. Kirill, the outlandish patriarch of the Russian Orthodox church, has called his presidency 'a miracle of God'; he and others have become willing supporters of the cult of war. No wonder the Christian church is trying to disown Russian orthodoxy.

"Kirill has declared the current war a Godly affair and praised the role it will play in keeping Russia safe from the horrors of gay-pride marches. More zealous churchmen have gone further.

"Elizbar Orlov, a priest in Rostov, a city close to the border with Ukraine, said the Russian army 'was cleaning the world of a diabolic infection'.

Antanov continues, "Putin has painted a world where the main culprits in this aggression are Britain and America—no longer remembered as allies in the fight against Nazis but cast instead as backers of the imaginary Nazis from which Ukraine must be saved."

He adds, "More important to the cult even than the priests are the siloviki of the security services, from whose ranks Mr Putin himself emerged. Officers of the FSB, one of the successors to the KGB, have been at the heart of Russian politics for 20 years. Like many inhabitants of closed, tightly knit, and powerful organisations, they tend to see themselves as members of a secret order with access to revealed truths denied to lesser folk. Anti-Westernism and a siege mentality are central to their beliefs. Mr Putin relies on the briefs with which they supply him, always contained in distinctive red folders, for his information about the world."

Christina remembers, "Just like Project Russia. The FSB delivered the book by courier services to various ministries dealing Russia's relationship with the world, warning them that democracy was a threat and the West an enemy."

Of course, the rest of the world just sat on its hands.

How to find Putin?

"With so many places to hide, how can we even find Putin?" I ask.

Charlie lists them out: His dacha in Ozero, his Palace, his Swiss ski lodge, the underground bunker in the Altai mountains, The Kremlin, his yacht, a plane?

Antanov adds, "There's also his command centre - The National Defense Control Center (NDCC) in Moscow - It is like a brightly lit version of the control bunker used by the Americans in that movie Dr Strangelove - But I doubt whether it would suit Putin to be holed up there. It is more the kind of place where he'd place his Generals."

He continued, "Putin is one for grandiose sets, big spaces with his courtiers in distant attendance. The yacht or plane don't sound too useful for that,"

Christina adds, "The ski lodge in Switzerland may be useful to park his family, out of harm's way, but I don't think he'd go there and if he did, then the news would certainly get out."

Charlie says, "So we are left with Ozero, where we were all a few days ago, his Palace and the underground bunker at Altai. I think we can rule out Ozero. I can't imagine Vitalievich and his buddies wouldn't know if Putin was holed up there."

Antanov says, "We've reduced it to a short list of two: The Palace on the Black Sea coast near Gelendzhik, Krasnodar Krai, and the bunker complex at Altayskoye Podvorie, in the Altai Mountains, on the River Katun."

Christina adds, "And we can't just follow Putin. There are his main followers, his absolute inner circle. We need to find out where they are."

Christina raises a good point. Vladimir Putin's Russia is not a one-man show. To understand how governance works, we will need to consider the power and complexity of the bureaucracy. Russia and Putin have been clever to tempt everyone to believe that Vladimir Putin makes all important decisions in Russia on his own. That politicians and bureaucrats then execute Putin's commands without fail in a system known as the 'power vertical;' and those political institutions serve merely to implement Putin's wishes.

This simplistic myth relates to how Russian decision-making is understood, to the implementation of decisions in Russia, and to the nature of the country's political institutions.

Putin's 'Direct Line' – an annual televised question-and-answer session during which the president hears from, and responds to, the problems of Russians across the country – combines all elements of the myth.

Putin appears to make decisions alone and, on the spot,

to solve callers' woes. He instructs officials to carry out these orders. And he engages directly with citizens, without the need for mediating institutions such as political parties or parliament.

To the extent that it reinforces misperceptions of Russia, this 'all-powerful Putin' myth can be framed in two ways. The 'positive' version – Putin as the 'good tsar' – suggests strong and competent leadership.

This myth makes Putin appear a more potent and unconstrained political force than is the case.

The 'negative' version of the myth, no less detrimental to a realistic understanding of Russian politics, highlights the pathologies of personalised decision-making and thus supports cartoonish Putin-as-dictator characterisations in the West.

Antanov speaks, "Since the Ukraine invasion began, Russian Defence Minister Sergei Shoigu and armed forces Chief of Staff Valery Gerasimov have become the central figures in Putin's war. For example, when Putin is not alone on the screen, they are usually around. Since the beginning of the Ukraine invasion, Shoigu and Gerasimov have become the faces of the war.

Christina adds, "The two are extremely close to Putin. They were Putin's military cortège during his television announcement on February 28 about having put Russia's nuclear forces on heightened alert. It is not surprising that the Kremlin decided to put Shoigu and Gerasimov in the spotlight. In Putin's eyes, they are the architects of the successful campaign to annex Crimea in 2014, Russia's military strategy in Syria as well as the support for the pro-Russian rebels in the Donbas region. They are also perceived to be being among the most loyal of

Putin's followers."

Antanov adds, " Shoigu wasn't even a full-time soldier. Some say he is the heir apparent to Putin. He is one of the rare members of the first circle of power to have had as much influence under Boris Yeltsin at the end of the 1990s as under Putin. He's a few years younger than Putin and began his political career at the end of the Soviet era, becoming defence minister in 2012 despite lacking military experience.

Christina speaks, "It is a peculiarity not uncommon under Putin, who is keen to keep senior officers out of this position. However, Shoigu also does not have any experience of the secret services, which is much less common among those close to Putin.

Antanov adds, "They say his great quality is that he is "a servant to the tsar and a father to soldiers,"

..."Or a 'perfect chameleon' capable of transforming himself at will to suit the pleasure of his leaders." adds Christina.

Antanov adds, "Shoigu is described as responsible for the fiction of the vast modernisation of the Russian army. As defence minister, Shoigu also supervised the feared Russian military intelligence service or GRU, which is suspected of having stepped up assassination operations in Europe in the 2010s, including poison attempts."

"Why the fiction of modernisation?" I ask.

Antanov answers, "They may have created ever more fearsome weapons, but they still run badly on old technology which has seldom been maintained. See a field of tank armour but know that only half of it can move and that a few of those units will have jammed guns."

"It's the same with their logistics. It may be boring to have to think about how to get supplies to the front - fuel, food, bullets etc., but without the supply chain the war grinds to a halt, just like that 40 km long Russian armoured convoy which ran out of fuel, " says Christina.

"Yes, it explains the lack of air superiority as well. A military force ill-prepared for an actual war," agreed Antanov.

"What about Valery Gerasimov?" asks Charlie.

"He's a career soldier," answers Antanov, "He served in the armoured divisions of the Red Army throughout the former Soviet Union."

"Gerasimov was also one of the commanders of the North Caucasus army during the second Chechen war (1999-2009). Anna Politkovskaya, a journalist who was gunned down in 2006 in her own apartment's elevator, called out the brutal methods of the Russian Army, including the threats they made toward their own troops.

Christina adds, "Gerasimov's international fame is based on a misunderstanding. He is said by some to be the inventor of Russian 'hybrid warfare', which combines the use of conventional weapons with non-military methods – such as disinformation or cyberattacks – to prepare the ground for soldiers. There is even a 'Gerasimov doctrine' named for this military approach. I had to learn some of it when I was being trained in Arkhangelsk. Gerasimov didn't invent it but he doesn't dispel the illusion."

Charlie speaks, "Okay, so we now have two sites to

watch and an additional two Generals to track."

"At least two, " says Antanov, "You know that the original 'Dead Hand' Perimeter systems are still running in Russia?"

I remembered this, but not that it was ever used. Like something out of villain central casting, the Soviet Union developed a world-ending mechanism that would launch all its nuclear weapons without any command from an actual human.

So called MAD - Mutually Assured Destruction.

Russia currently has an estimated 1,600 deployed tactical nuclear weapons, with another 2,400 strategic nuclear weapons tied to intercontinental ballistic missiles. This makes Russia the largest nuclear power in the world. All of these weapons are tied into the Perimeter, an automatic nuclear weapons control system.

In a crisis that might mean a first strike from the United States, high-ranking government officials or military commanders could activate the Perimeter. Perimeter would guarantee that the Soviet Union (and now, Russia) could respond even if its entire armed forces were wiped out.

Once switched on, the Perimeter system can launch the entire Russian nuclear arsenal in response to a nuclear attack. It was part of the Cold War doctrine of mutually assured destruction, a means of deterring nuclear attacks by ensuring the side who initiated a first strike also would be annihilated.

Called "Dead Hand" in the West, the theory is that a command and control system measures communications on military frequencies, radiation levels, air pressure, heat, and short-term seismic disturbances. If the measurement points to a nuclear attack, the Perimeter begins a sequence that would end in the firing of all ICBMs in the Russian arsenal.

Perimeter would launch a command rocket, tipped with a radio warhead that transmits launch orders to Russian nuclear silos, even with the presence of radio jamming. The rocket would fly across the entire length of the country. After several test launches to prove the viability of such a command rocket, the Perimeter system went online in 1985.

The Soviet Union never confirmed that such a system ever existed, but Russian Strategic Missile Forces General Sergey Karakaev confirmed it to a Russian newspaper in 2011, saying the U.S. could be destroyed in 30 minutes. Russian state media outlets suggest the system was upgraded to include radar early warning systems and Russia's new hypersonic missiles.

In the United States, similar technologies were developed. Seismic and radiation sensors are used to monitor parts of the U.S. and the world for nuclear explosions and other activity, but the U.S. military never created an automatic trigger for its arsenal. Instead, it ensured that American humans with the ability and authority to launch a second strike would survive a first strike.

Since the Perimeter is still active, the danger of an automatic, computer-generated nuclear strike still exists. Now that Russian President Vladimir Putin has put Russia's nuclear weapons on high alert, he might have placed Russia's doomsday device on notice as well.

"This is where Antanov and I can assist," says Christina, "It is risky, but I can ask Blackbird for their location. They must have a command centre somewhere, and it is presumably close to Putin."

"Okay," says Antanov, "I guess we will need to reconvene in the morning, when Blackbird can give us some direction."

Blackbird

The next morning, we all assemble in Christina's suite again. She explains she had been able to contact Fyodor Kuznetsov, her handler, codenamed Blackbird.

Christina made the call with Antanov, who was also run by Blackbird. Christina explains that she has 'left' the FSB now, although Antanov continues to have a role.

"It is delicate, because Kuznetsov will want to remain cautious, although he trusts me and Antanov implicitly," she explains.

Antanov nods, "It would have been very difficult to ask him if he could help locate Vladimir Putin, Sergei Shoigu and Valery Gerasimov. Blackbird is smart and would know instantly why we were asking."

Christina explains, "Yes, but Blackbird has not been impressed with the current regime, since before Serbia, when Russia rolled in for a take-over. He could see Putin was beginning to lose perspective, even then."

Christina looks around the room and then continues, "I didn't ask him a direct question, because I could tell he was worried. Blackbird is caught between loyalty and distaste for the current regime.

Now he is less well-regarded by the Kremlin, it would have put him in danger if I'd asked him directly about Putin."

"Instead, I asked him for the whereabout of my old

friends, Irina Morozova and Eckhart Bloch, from Saint Petersburg. He didn't know but said he would text me. About half an hour later I received a number. It began with '+7 727' and I realised they must still be in Saint Petersburg. "

"I called the number and it was answered after three rings!"

"Irina thought it was a hoax to begin with - me calling them - but then she realised it was really me when I started to talk about the rock-concert trip we all did together. I checked their current links into the Russian establishment, but they have both left the Service. It was all part of a planned exit when I worked with them several years ago. But that is a whole other story."

"I remembered how well wired-up Saint Petersburg is and so I had to explain our purpose to them in a kind of conversational code. Well, the good news is that they will be in on our plan and decided of their own will to come to Cyprus and to meet us. True to form they both had 'Go-Bags' ready and decided to make the last plane yesterday to Moscow and then to catch the once-a-day service here to Cyprus. It lands this afternoon in Paphos!"

"They must be some really good friends," said Charlie.

"Oh - they are the best," said Christina.

Antanov nodded, "I'd better call Artem, to get us a ride to Paphos - I think it is around 70 kilometres west of here."

Irina and Eckhart

Later, we walk out to the familiar sight of Artem's taxi, and climbed in. We struck lucky with Artem and his wonderfully air-conditioned taxi, and he told us that the journey should take less than an hour, because the road we would travel was the Limassol – Paphos highway, a modern four-lane, high-speed route. It links Limassol, the largest port, and Paphos, the top tourist destination on the island.

Soon enough we're on the road, which reminded me of a brand-new English dual-carriageway complete with white writing on green signage, except it was bathed in permanent sunshine. Artem told us that the road had a maximum speed limit of 100 km per hour, but also a minimum limit of 65 km per hour.

"I'll pick up your friends and then take you all to the beach in Paphos. There are some lovely restaurants along the waterfront," declares Artem.

I wondered how many of them were run by members of his family.

We soon arrive at the small airport, which appears to be a single terminal, although Artem is telling us all that there is another older terminal as well. He seemed to know his way around and is waved to by several of the staff. Then he produces an iPad from the front of the van and types in 'Irina Morozova' - which appears in big letters on the front of the iPad. He adds 'Eckhart Bloch' and then walks out into the terminal, reassuringly saying, "It's okay here," leaving us all in the minivan parked in a loading zone.

We work out that Irina and Eckhart would have arrived around 20 minutes ago. Sure enough, he quickly returns, with two extra people in tow.

"My god!" says Christina and runs to greet first Irina and then Eckhart. There is much rapid chattering as they reacquaint. I can see they are all good friends, if somewhat distant. Antanov does the same at a more leisurely pace and all four re-board the minibus with big grins.

"Let me introduce you to the others!" announces Christina and in turn we all say 'hello' and greet one another.

"Right," says Artem, "Now I take you to my cousin's wonderful bar on the waterfront in Paphos. It will take about 20 minutes. I will leave you there and maybe Charlie can call me when you want to leave."

We all agree this is a good plan and before we know it, we are climbing from the minibus into the hot sunshine and making our way to a balcony bar which overlooks the Mediterranean. There are screens above our head making the whole restaurant seem cool compared to the ambient temperature.

"Artem, this is perfect," says Charlie, and the rest of us nod in agreement.

"I called ahead to ask them to give you a good table and view, " says Artem, as they show us to a corner area which looks out onto the sea. I still can't get over the green sky, which is making the sea look green as well.

"Remember," says Artem, "Just call me and I'll be here in about 10 minutes!"

"Christina Nott! I had forgotten just how much travelling with you is always an adventure!" says Eckhart.

"This time we are right in the middle of something - Oh and thank you for coming along - you must have been in transit for hours!"

"It was a couple of flights; to Moscow and then to here, although the flight to Paphos was on a holiday plane!" answers Eckhart.

"Maybe this will be a holiday for us!" answered Irina, "So what has been happening?"

Christina and sometimes Antanov regale Irina and Eckhart with the story of how we all came to Cyprus, and what we are doing. Eckhart is particularly interested when we mention the Tupolev plane. Christina doesn't mention the unusual qualities that Charlie, Chantal and I possess.

"So, what do you think you need us for?" asks Irina, "You know already that we can be more than backup singers!"

Irina explains

"It's crazy in Russia now," Irina explains, "Most of us don't like what Putin is doing, and none of us can see it ending well. It is destroying our economy, our reputation and many of the wealthy Russians are losing money so quickly they cannot believe it."

Irina continues with a jaded voice, "Russian television is filled with propaganda, the independent channels have closed down and foreign channels are blocked. By some technicality, the Al Jazeera service in English is still getting through, and that's where we and many Russians are getting news."

Eckhart explains, "To give a sense of Putin's reach, after he jailed the leader of Russia's opposition, Alexei Navalny, we hear that Navalny has just been sentenced to another nine years imprisonment. Putin is a loose cannon. He surprised his generals with a war, is telling the mass of Russians a different story and has silenced his opposition party.

"Navalny will probably be moved from Vladimir, where he has been kept for more than a year, to a yet harsher maximum-security jail elsewhere. The crime for which he was sentenced is a trumped up one of fraud.

Eckhart continues, "We have the parallel that the Ukrainians want to embrace many, if not all, the values held dear by other European nations. Mr Navalny wants the same for Russia. Vladimir Putin cannot countenance either ambition and has made up a phoney excuse to go on a disgusting and violent bombing campaign against civilians."

Irina says, "Yes, Putin sees himself like a modern-day crusader against the liberal future offered in Europe. He is fighting in the name of Russkiy mir — 'the Russian world', that obscure historical term for a Slavic civilisation based on shared ethnicity, religion, and heritage.

"Putin's regime has revived, promulgated and debased this idea into an obscurantist anti-Western mixture of Orthodox dogma, nationalism, conspiracy theory and security-state Stalinism.

Irina continues, "You must remember, Christina, when we talked about Putin's rise, back when we sat in Literaturnoye Kafe in Saint Petersburg? It's just more of the same gangsterism, but now he has the overt power to swagger through with his crazy plans. His inner circles fear him. If they don't do what he says, they'll end up in a prison camp or their families will disappear."

Eckhart speaks, "Though Putin's ascension to the presidency in 2000 was helped by his willingness to wage war in Chechnya, his mandate was to stabilise an economy still reeling from the debt crisis of 1998 and to consolidate the gains, mostly pocketed by oligarchs, of the first post-Soviet decade.

Eckhart adds, "Putin's contract with the Russian people

was based not on religion or ideology, but on improving incomes. His new ideology of isolationism appeared in some of the darker corners of the power structure. It took two years before his new way of thinking became obvious to the outside world. His Munich speech in 2007 was when Putin formally rejected the idea of Russia's integration into the West. He went so far as to tell a press conference in Moscow that nuclear weapons and Orthodox Christianity were the two pillars of Russian society, the one guaranteeing the country's external security, the other its moral health."

"This was around the time I wanted to get out," said Christina, "You know, from the life, the FSB, all of it."

"And it is when I met you in Saint Petersburg, and you had already secured financial freedom and were using that 'one last job' to guarantee it," said Irina.

"It was shortly before the 'Snow Revolution' that we did that Tour," said Eckhart, "I can remember thinking 'What would Christina do?' during that time - but of course, you had gone..."

"Ah yes, I watched the Snow Revolution unfold from afar," answered Christina, "I was worried about Russia at that time, as Putin's madness and faux-ideology crept over the entire Motherland."

Eckhart continues, "Both Irina and I were still attached to the FSB at that time. We were not able to fully engineer our escape for another couple of years. Fortunately, in Russia, money talks. "

He adds, "The Snow Revolution began as protests against the Russian legislative election results. You remember, the vote stuffing and so on. They were motivated by claims by Russian and foreign journalists, political activists, and members of the public that the election process was deeply flawed and being run by gangsters.

"After a week of small-scale demonstrations, Russia saw some of the biggest protests in Moscow since the 1990s. The focus of the protests was against the ruling party, United Russia, and its leader Vladimir Putin, the current president, previous prime minister, and previous two-term president, who announced his intention to run again for President in 2012.

Irina adds, "Then, another round of large protests took place. They were named "For Fair Elections" and their organizers set up the movement of the same name. Initial protest actions, organised by the leaders of the Russian opposition parties and non-systemic opposition sparked fear in some quarters of anti-regime protest movements and an accompanying change of government."

Eckart adds, "This is when it became complicated! On the first days following the election, Putin and United Russia were supported by rallies of two youth organisations, the government-organised Nashi, and United Russia's Young Guard. They set about confusing everyone by running counter-protests."

He continues, "On 24 December Sergey Kurginyan organised the first protest against what was viewed as "orange" protesters in Moscow, though the protest also went under the same slogan "For Fair Elections".

Irina speaks, "By the following February, more protests and pro-government rallies were held throughout Russia. The largest events were in Moscow: the 'anti-Orange protest' (alluding to the Orange Revolution in Ukraine), aimed against 'orangism', 'collapse of the country', 'perestroika' and 'revolution'. Putin kept using that motif right through to the start of the bombardment of Ukraine."

Eckhart adds, "By 6 May 2012, protests took place in Moscow against rigged elections. It was the day before Putin's inauguration as President for his third term. Some called for the inauguration to be scrapped. The protests were marred by violence between the protesters and the police. About 400 protesters were arrested, including Alexei Navalny, Boris Nemtsov, and Sergei Udaltsov and around 100 were injured. On the day of the inauguration, 7 May, over 100 protesters were arrested in Moscow so that in June 2012, laws were enacted which set strict boundaries on protests and imposed heavy penalties for unauthorised actions.

Irina adds, "I can remember, around that time, that Alexei Navalny spoke and was greeted with an ovation. He said there were enough people present at the protest to overrun the Kremlin, but that they were committed to remaining peaceful, at least for the moment. I copied his speech to my phone at the time, and here it is:

"I can see that there are enough people here to seize the Kremlin and the Moscow White House right now. We are a peaceful force and will not do it now. But if these crooks and thieves try to go on cheating us, if they continue telling lies and stealing from us, we will take what belongs to us with our own hands. ... These days, with the help of the zombie-box (TV), they are trying to prove to us that they are big and scary beasts. But we know who they are. Little sneaky jackals! Is that right? Is that true or not?' "

Now Antanov speaks, "There it was: the last act of defiance before Putin tightened the screws on everything. After a hearing a message of 'Russia without

Putin' the securocrats and clerics started to expand their dogma into daily life."

Irina adds, "Like in Saint Petersburg years before, it quickly became a regime which sustained networks of corruption, rent extraction and extortion required religion and an ideology of national greatness to restore the legitimacy lost during the looting. "

Eckhart says, "Navalny showed a video of Putin's palace near Sochi - which Putin has since denied owning."

Antanov adds, "Yes. Covering up things of such size requires a lot of ideology. At that point it was still possible to see the ideology as a smokescreen rather than a product of real belief. Perhaps that was a mistake; perhaps the underlying reality changed."

I thought that, either way, the onset of the Covid-19 pandemic brought a raising of the ideological stakes. Putin arranged constitutional changes which removed all limits on his term in office. His people also installed new ideological norms: gay marriage was banned, Russian was enshrined as the 'language of the state-forming people' and God given an official place in the nation's heritage.

Eckhart says, "Putin's long periods of isolation sees him become preoccupied with history, paying particular heed to figures like Konstantin Leontyev, an ultra-reactionary 19th-century visionary who admired hierarchy and monarchy, cringed at democratic uniformity, and believed in the freezing of time.

He adds, "Putin spends much time with Yuri Kovalchuk, a close friend who controls a vast media group. According to Russian journalists they discussed Mr

Putin's mission to restore unity between Russia and Ukraine. Hence a war against Ukraine which is also a war against Russia's future—or at least the future as it has been conceived of by the Russia's sometimes small but frequently dominant Westernising faction for the past 350 years."

I think about all of this. Putin's war is intended to wipe out the possibility of any future that looks towards Europe and a liberal modernity. In Ukraine there would be no coherent future left in its place. In Russia, the modernisers would leave as their already diminished world was replaced by something fiercely reactionary and inward-looking.

He is building a new iron curtain and the countries such as Ukraine and Belarus become the buffer zones. No wonder there is much discussion of which could become members of NATO, and of Latvia and Estonia already on the inside.

The Russian-backed republics in Donetsk and Luhansk become a subverted model. There, like in the old days in Dresden or Saint Petersburg, crooks and thugs are elevated to unaccustomed status, armed with new weapons, and fitted with allegedly glorious purpose: to fight against Ukraine's European dream. In Russia they would be tasked with keeping any such dream from returning, whether from abroad, or from within a cell.

Дедовщина

Дедовщина Dedovshchina

Dedovshchina: literally: reign of grandfathers is the informal practice of hazing and abuse of junior conscripts historically in the Soviet Armed Forces and today in the Russian armed forces, internal troops, and to a much lesser extent FSB, border guards, as well as the military forces of certain former Soviet Republics. It consists of brutalisation by more senior conscripts, NCOs, and officers.

Dedovshchina encompasses a variety of subordinating and humiliating activities undertaken by the junior ranks, from doing the chores of the senior ranks, to violent and sometimes deadly physical and psychological abuse, not unlike an extremely vicious form of bullying or torture, including sexual torture and rape. When not leaving the army seriously injured, conscripts can suffer serious mental trauma for their lifetime. It is often cited by former military personnel as a major source of poor morale.

Often with the justification of maintaining authority, physical violence or psychological abuse can be used to make the "youth" do certain fatiguing duties. In many situations, hazing is not the goal, and senior conscripts exploit their juniors in order to provide themselves with a more comfortable existence, akin to slavery, and the violent aspects arise when juniors refuse. There have been occasions where soldiers have been seriously injured or killed.

From Wikipedia, the free encyclopaedia

Big Story

Now it was Eckhart's turn to speak.

"This is a very big story. But it's not only about Ukraine. It's about the world, about the politicians of the world and I think we can speak about it after Ukraine wins. On one level it's not about who has more weapons or more money or gas or oil.

"That's the very first thing that I understood, when Russia made a move on Crimea in 2014. I was tasked with a security job over there as part of the FSB but wearing an unmarked Russian uniform. In fact, most of the Russian troops deployed were not wearing any form of identification. Within hours of the treaty's signing, a Ukrainian soldier was killed when masked gunmen stormed a Ukrainian military base outside Simferopol.

"I knew we'd all been through clandestine training, but this was wholesale deception, by not showing our true colours to the Ukrainians running Crimea. I thought we behaved like cowards."

Eckhart continues, "Russian troops moved to occupy bases throughout the peninsula, including the Ukrainian naval headquarters in Sevastopol, as Ukraine initiated the evacuation of some 25,000 military personnel and their families from Crimea. On 21 March, after the ratification of the annexation treaty by the Russian parliament, Putin signed a law formally integrating

Crimea into Russia.

"As international attention remained focused on Crimea, Yatsenyuk, the head of Ukrainian Economy and later Ukraine's Prime Minister negotiated with the IMF to craft a bailout package that would address Ukraine's $35 billion in unmet financial obligations.

"He also met with EU officials in Brussels, and on 21 March Yatsenyuk signed a portion of the association pact that had been rejected by the previous leader Yanukovych in November 2013.

"The IMF ultimately proposed an $18 billion loan package that was contingent on Ukraine's adoption of a range of austerity measures that included devaluation of the Hryvnya and curbs on state subsidies that reduced the price of natural gas to consumers.

Eckhart sighs, "I honestly thought Yatsenyuk was fighting Ukraine's corner, even after the overrunning of Serbia. He spoke out against Russia, tried to get Ukraine funding and was trying to position for EU-acceptance of Ukraine.

Antanov speaks, "I remember this. Yatsenyuk was smeared in a political campaign run by Oleksandr Onyshchenko, former Ukrainian MP. Onyshchenko admitted to the UK's Independent newspaper that he organised and funded a US$30 million smear campaign against Yatsenyuk and his government, playing on a corruption line. Russia's National Bureau of Interpol requested that Yatsenyuk be put on the international wanted list alleging his violation of articles of the Criminal Code of Russia.

"In other words, Russia wanted to get Yatsenyuk back

under their control in a cell. I remember because we were all sent the bulletin."

Irina speaks, "Volodymyr Zelensky is the current leader of Ukraine and has strong spirit. He also says that Ukraine can't be part of somebody else. He says that Ukrainians are the same as people in the USA and Europe and Russia. He says it's not about who has more weapons or more money or gas or oil.

She adds, "Zelensky sees that some politicians live in an information vacuum. What we see is that this is a closed atmosphere with Putin now. It means Putin can't understand or he couldn't know what's going on outside. Now we see a Putin obsessed with his dream of being a mini-tsar.

Eckhart starts again, "Yes, but pre-emptive sanctions would have given more time to Ukraine's military to prepare for Russia's further invasion. They would have shown Belarus what could happen if pre-emptive sanctions involving Russian businesses, oil, and gas exports, and more were taken, and this considering that Belarusians do not support Russia's war against Ukraine.

Irina adds, "Zelensky raised the Nord Stream 2 pipeline with Biden and Merkel, when she was still in office, and later with Scholz. He said the first step will be to launch it, then Russia will block gas supplies to Ukraine, and next they will apply pressure, including on Moldova, and then Russia will block supplies to split countries within the EU. Like a gangster drug dealer, they know how to apply pressure."

Eckhart again, "Even now, weeks into the conflict, western partners have still not completed the sanctions on disconnecting the banking system from SWIFT, many more banks have not been disconnected. Much fuss is made but less happens. They have taken very important steps to support Ukraine, but the central bank of Russia has not been disconnected. They say they will impose an embargo on Russian oil and gas exports. All these sanctions are incomplete. They have been threatened, but not yet implemented.

Eckhart sounds angry, "They also kick the triggers for action along the road. Now we are hearing those certain decisions depend on whether Russia launches a chemical attack on Ukraine. It's disgusting. As if they think that Ukrainians are like so many guinea pigs to be experimented on."

Christina speaks, "Many countries view Russia now through a military-strategic lens and are using Ukraine as a shield. It is good that they are on the side of Ukraine, but they must stop being defensive in their dialogue with Russia. They can act offensively. SWIFT is still operating in Russia for the leaders of Russia. Don't forget that ordinary Russians are now isolated, deprived of information. They don't know what's going on.

Eckhart's voice is still angry, "Ukrainian people are dying. Russian people don't know what's going on. They don't understand. Social media have been shut down and a lot of people are watching state-run television. It's a big problem because the Kremlin controls all levels of power and all this information. And it is painting the Russian people as co-conspirators."

Irina adds, "Meanwhile, the Russians block supplies to Mariupol, Melitopol, Berdyansk, Kherson, Kharkiv, but they're not in the bigger cities. And what do they do? In Melitopol and Berdyansk they are switching to roubles.

"They are kidnapping the mayors of the cities. They killed some of them. Some of them can't be found. Some of them are dead.

"Most of the Russian military are scared, they are operating under Dedovshchina rules, where they are bullied, frightened and harassed. It is no way to run the military."

Eckhart adds, "And some of them were replaced. They are doing the same thing that they did in Donbas in 2014. The same people are carrying out these operations. It's the same methodology. The West can't say, 'We'll help you in the weeks to come.' It doesn't allow Ukraine to unblock Russian-occupied cities, to bring food to residents there. People are simply not able to get out. There is no food, medicine or drinking water there. Some small cities have been destroyed. There are no people and no houses. All that's left is the name.

Christina says, "Putin knows that many western politicians are afraid of him and therefore afraid of Russia."

Eckhart nods, "That is right. Everyone has varied interests. There are those in the West who don't mind a long war because it would mean exhausting Russia, even if this means the demise of Ukraine and comes at the cost of Ukrainian lives.

Christina adds, "This is definitely in the interests of some countries. For other countries, it would be better if the war ended quickly, because Russia's market is a big one that their economies are suffering because of the war.

Antanov speaks, "From the west, Ukraine needs aeroplanes, tanks and armoured personnel vehicles.

They don't have as many as they need. The Russians have thousands of military vehicles, and they are coming and coming and coming.

Christina summarises, "Putin has a 20th-century view of a 21st-century country."

"If that!" says Eckhart, "I'd say it was almost a 'Middle-Ages' mentality. The invaders do not even mourn their own casualties. This is something I do not understand. Some 15,000 Russian soldiers have been killed in one month. Ukrainians talk about a war that has lasted for eight years. Eight years!"

Eckhart continues, "And in eight years, Ukraine also lost 15,000 lives. And Russia loses 15,000 of its soldiers in a month! Putin is throwing inexperienced Russian soldiers like logs into a train's furnace. And they are not even burying them. Their corpses are left in the streets. In several small cities soldiers say it's impossible to breathe because of the smell. It is the stench of rotting flesh."

Antanov speaks, "Ukrainian soldiers defended Mariupol. They could have left if they wanted. But there were still others alive in the city along with their wounded. And then there were the dead, the fallen comrades. Ukraine's defenders say they must stay and bury those killed in action and save the lives of those wounded in action. If people are still alive, the Ukrainian army must continue to protect them. And this is the fundamental difference between the way the opposing sides in this war see the world."

I'm aware that most of this conversation has been between four Russians, all ashamed of their country's actions driven through fear by an increasingly isolated Putin.

Chantal describes the situation

Chantal summarises:

"We can't be certain this whole situation is being driven by Putin. Certainly, The Kremlin is making it look that way, but it could be to throw us off balance. Putin also has many bases for operation. We are trying to rule some of them out. There's his dacha in Ozero, his Palace at Krasnodar Krai, his Swiss ski lodge, the underground bunker in the Altai mountains, The Kremlin, his yacht, a plane, and the National Defense Control Center in Moscow."

Irina smiles, "Well, that is easy. It must be the place that the least people know about, ideally protected from air strikes. He will be at the bunker complex at Altayskoye Podvorie, in the Altai Mountains, on the River Katun."

Eckhart nods in agreement, "Yes, crazy as it may seem, Putin will have picked the bunker complex. It is incredibly well provisioned and most of it is underground. They brought in special German tunnelling equipment when they built it, and they used Dostoyevskaya on the Lyublinsko-Dmitrovskaya Metro Line as a motif during construction. Don't think of rough chiselled walls, instead think of a shiny metro station. Putin tries so hard to copy Stalin. His bunker is like the metro stations Stalin had built all over Moscow. "

"How do you know all of this?" asks Charlie.

"I was one of his protection officers back in the day," explains Eckhart.

"Christina. You know some interesting people," says Charlie.

"The scary thing about Putin was his developing craziness," adds Eckhart.

"We were told about this by Dr Maria Gvasalia, when we were at a meeting with Svalov Rollan Vitalievich," answers Christina.

"Vitalievich?" asks Irina, "Is he still alive?"

"Very much so when we saw him, but I can't be sure what happened when a truckload of gun carrying heavies arrived at his Dacha in Ozero," answers Christina, "in fact, Vitalievich was planning a hit on Putin."

"Well Putin is extremely paranoid, also," says Eckhart, "He will probably be wearing the latest personal armour. If you see him now, outside in public, like at the Luzhniki stadium, he will be wearing big bulky clothes. Not because it is cold, so much as because of the protection it offers. He distracts the message by wearing a 1.5 million rouble coat, and a 350 thousand rouble sweater. The press are more interested to find out it comes from Loro Piana than whether or not he has Kevlar underneath."

"Well, we think that the Russian elite are plotting to

poison Putin," explains Irina, "There would be a wry sense of irony if they did, after it is what he ordered for so many of his enemies."

Eckhart says, "It is why spy chief Oleksandr Bortnikov, head of the FSB agency, was removed. He was once thought to have been lined up as Putin's replacement. He used to be a top sidekick of the president, but 70-year-old Bortnikov is said to have fallen out of favour over 'fatal miscalculations' in the conflict with Kyiv.

"Putin's Chief Directorate of Intelligence said: 'It is known that Bortnikov and some other influential representatives of the Russian elite are considering various options to remove Putin from power. In particular, poisoning, sudden disease or any other coincidence is not excluded.'"

Christina comments, "But that is so much more difficult to do, than, say a close-range bullet, or an explosion."

"Not necessarily," answered Eckhart, "You remember that I was a protection officer? When they excavated Altayskoye Podvorie they also had to install hundreds of kilometres of HVAC. Heating, Ventilation and Air Conditioning. The difference with the HVAC used in Altayskoye Podvorie is that they built in security too. The Central Air Handling Unit could also pump a blend of other mixture around the system, or a selected part. It was designed as a ring defence for the whole complex. The outer rings, if breached, could inject a toxin into the HVAC, which would destroy incoming marauders in a similar manner to the boiling oil used in bygone times."

Irina adds, "It would be a little more subtle than the head-on attack planned by Vitalievich and could even be made to look like an accident."

Eckhart agrees, "There's a battle inside the Kremlin even in advance of Vladimir Putin's departure from office, with claims that the president presides over a secret multibillion-dollar fortune.

"Rival clans inside the Kremlin are embroiled in a struggle for the control of assets as Putin prepares to transfer power to his hand-picked successor, Dmitry Anatolyevich Medvedev.

Eckhart continues, "Western observers widely believed Medvedev was too liberal and too pro-Western for Putin to endorse as a candidate. Instead, they expected the candidate to arise from the ranks of the so-called siloviki, security and military officials many of whom were appointed to high positions during Putin's presidency. The silovik Sergei Ivanov and the administrator-specialist Viktor Zubkov were seen as the strongest candidates. We still don't know exactly why Putin proposed Medvedev although I guess at stake are billions of dollars in assets belonging to Russian state-run corporations. Additionally, details of Putin's own personal fortune, reportedly hidden in Switzerland and Liechtenstein, are being discussed for the first time. It's the siloviki vs the liberal clan, of which Medvedev is a member.

Irina says, "After eight years in power Putin has secretly accumulated more than $40bn (£20bn). The sum would make him Russia's - and Europe's - richest man.

"Putin owns vast holdings in three Russian oil and gas companies, concealed behind a "non-transparent network of offshore trusts".

Eckhart says, "Irina is right: Putin's name doesn't appear

on any shareholders' register, of course. The scheme is of successive ownership of offshore companies and funds with a final point buried in Zug, Switzerland, and Liechtenstein.

Irina says, "Discussion of Putin's wealth has previously been taboo. But the claims have leaked out against the backdrop of a fight inside the Kremlin between a group led by Igor Sechin, Putin's influential deputy chief of staff, and a "liberal" clan that includes Medvedev.

"The Sechin group is made up of siloviki - Kremlin officials with security/military backgrounds. It is said to include Nikolai Patrushev, the head of the Federal Security Service (FSB), his deputy Alexander Bortnikov, and Putin's aide Viktor Ivanov. I find it difficult to believe that Putin would favour the liberals over the siloviki, although that seems to be the outward appearance."

Christina queries, "Well maybe that is the idea. We know Putin is a master of deception and lies. Perhaps this is to keep everyone guessing?"

Eckhart adds, "Those associated with the liberal camp include Roman Abramovich, the Russian oligarch once the direct owner of Chelsea football club who is close to Putin and the Yeltsin family. Other members are Viktor Cherkesov, the head of the federal drug control service, and Alisher Usmanov, an Uzbek-born billionaire."

"And Abramovich has already been targeted in a most silovik manner," says Irina.

Christina adds, "I doubt the struggle has much to do with ideology. It is a war between business competitors. Putin's decision to endorse Medvedev as president - who has no links with the secret services - dealt a severe blow to the hardline Sechin clan - it will soon be full-on bratva wars all over again."

Irina adds, "Some analysts have said Putin would like to retire but has been forced to carry on in order to shield Medvedev from siloviki plotting. Others say Putin wants to stay in power. There is no secret any longer about his cancer nor about the steroids he is receiving as treatment.

I surmise Putin could be running interference to make things seem very uncertain for everyone.

"The siloviki are not nice," said Christina, "They play like tough and ruthless gangsters - exactly the way Putin himself used to operate"

"Used to?" queries Charlie, "His current actions seem no different."

Christina adds, "The wave of re-nationalisations under Putin transformed Putin's associates into multimillionaires. The dilemma now facing the Kremlin's elite is how to hang on to its wealth if Putin leaves power. Most of its money is located in the west. The pressing problem is how to protect these funds from any future administration that may seek to reclaim them?"

Eckhart adds, "Yes, the first hints of the intra-clan warfare gripping the Kremlin emerged when the FSB arrested General Alexander Bulbov, the deputy head of the federal drug agency, and part of the liberal group. His arrest saw a surreal standoff, with his bodyguards and FSB agents pointing machine guns at each other. Sergei Storchak - another liberal - was also arrested and charged with embezzling $43.4m. He is currently in prison."

Irina adds, "But the liberal group - one of several competing factions inside the Kremlin - has struck back. Oleg Shvartsman, a previously obscure fund manager, gave an interview to Kommersant newspaper claiming he secretly managed the finances of a group of FSB officers. These officers were involved in 'velvet reprivatisations', - in effect forcibly acquiring private companies at below-market value and transforming them into state-owned firms. The assets were redistributed via offshore companies."

Christina looks agitated, "But these are the same moves that Putin did in Sankt Petersburg and during his early days in Moscow!"

"Correct," said Eckhart, "The randomised corruption of the 1990s has given way to the systemic and institutionalised corruption of the Putin era. Members of Putin's cabinet personally control the most important sectors of the economy - oil, gas, and defence. Medvedev is chairman of Gazprom; Sechin runs Rosneft; other ministers are chairmen of Russian railways, Aeroflot, a nuclear fuel giant and an energy transport enterprise. Putin has created a new, more streamlined oligarchy where the crown jewels of the country's wealth have ended up in the hands of Putin's inner circle,"

"You know something?" says Eckhart, "Gazprom Neft built Putin's bunker in the Altai Mountains, The above surface version of it looks like a luxury resort. Above ground is maybe one tenth the size of the underground complex. And you know who is the owner of Gazprom? Alexander Ivanovich Medvedev! Wheels within wheels."

Irina adds, "And Roman Abramovich and Boris

Berezovsky acquired the Gazprom Neft for a knock down US$100 million, after bidding through several front companies that had been set up for this specific purpose. It is worth $35.2 billion now. That is some return."

"Crooked return?" queries Christina, "Even Blackbird thinks that the west has misunderstood Putin. Everyone has been distracted by his 'neo-Soviet' image. Putin is ultimately a 'classic' businessman who believes money can solve any problem, and whose psychology was shaped by his experiences working in the St Petersburg mayor's office in Russia's crime-ridden early 1990s."

Antanov says, "We shouldn't forget the degree to which the west was taken in by Putin. In 2007, he was Time Magazine's Person of the year and even in 2014 he was short-listed as a runner-up."

Eckhart adds, "An unprecedented silent battle is taking place inside the Kremlin in advance of Vladimir Putin's departure from office with claims that the president presides over a secret multibillion-dollar fortune."

Charlie tries to summarise, "So, I get it: Rival clans inside the Kremlin are embroiled in a struggle for the control of assets as Putin prepares to transfer power to a hand-picked successor. And now we see a new Iron Curtain is grinding into place. As Ukraine bears the brunt of heavy bombing, we can also see an economic war deepening as the military conflict escalates and civilian casualties rise."

Drones

"So how can we formulate a multi-point attack?" asks Charlie, "We'll need to deploy the drones as well."

I suggest, "Maybe we need our 'mistress of chaos', our shapeshifter and a couple of military people to go along to Geçitkale Airbase?"

"Good plan, and we'll need Artem to ferry us to the base, " answered Christina.

"At this stage, all we need to do is convince them that they have weapons which they can validly deploy," says Eckhart.

"Maybe I'll need that NATO uniform again?" asks Chantal.

"I think I might need one, actually," asserts Christina, "I'll know all the ranks and the terminology. I won't get caught out," she explains, "Besides, I know how to wear the beret correctly."

Antanov chuckles, both he and Christina had noticed a few uniform infractions when Chantel had been clothed by Charlie.

I notice Chantal look relieved at this news, but also that Charlie is ready for action. It looks as if Christina will be the high-ranking leader, with Antanov, Charlie and me as backup. I'm beginning to learn about being in Christina's band.

Artem is to drive us to the base, which is right at the other end of Cyprus in Turkish territory.

First Artem takes Irina, Eckhart, and Chantal back to our apartment block, and then drives the rest of us to Geçitkale, in Turkish Cyprus. I wonder about the border crossing, but Artem says everything will be simple.

Artem estimated 3 hours to cover the 200 kilometres to the airbase. But we have good traffic and the last section from Limassol to the airbase takes about an hour and a half.

Artem was also correct about the border crossing. We had to put a white paper into our passport to have it stamped, with our corresponding passport number. Artem had to show minibus insurance and then we were on our way and soon at the airbase.

This is where Christina takes control and with her Turkish NATO uniform directs us all to the entrance to the facility. Charlie pulls a couple of shapeshifts to get us through the barriers and we are then inside, driving along in Artem's minibus.

He has been to the base many times and knows the way to the main building. We disembark and Christina requests to see the Airbase Commander. She is speaking English now, but her NATO rank and beret are helpful and we are soon whisked into a holding lobby.

She explains that Charlie and I are civilians and Antanov, is a Colonel, but in plain clothes. She explains that I am a lawyer, sent to ensure that the entire process is legally executed. Charlie is a non-specific NATO representative. We have been tasked with gaining agreement that the Turkish NATO Bayraktar TB2s can be deployed, but that there is no immediate call for action.

Christina's Tümgeneral rank is a NATO OF-7, which is higher than the base commander, who is the Turkish rank of Albay or Colonel, which has more stars but is a lower rank of NATO OF-5. Christina asserts her demands, in English, to the surprised Commander, who, with a graceful dignity agrees to everything. It is clear t base has never seen such a powerful woman officer in their military, nor are they used to conducting business in English.

There are a few administrative details to clear up, but Christina's assertions with her clearly superior rank is all that is needed for us to have mobilised a significant air threat, which is poised but won't do anything without further orders.

Christina gestures for us to leave and we back out of the meeting room and into Artem's waiting minibus. He sedately pulls away as we all look at one another.

"We did it," says Christina, "I did lay it on pretty heavy and explained that failure to accept the order would be a court-martial offence. That's why I was travelling with a lawyer. What is happening is unprecedented and so people don't really know how to act. We now have the whole airbase ready to activate their Bayraktar drones on our instructions."

بث الأخبار

bathu al'akhbar
Doha, Qatar
English version

KYIV, Ukraine — President Recep Tayyip Erdogan of Turkey agreed to expand supplies of one of the Ukrainian Army's most sophisticated weapons, a long-range, Turkish-made armed drone whose use in combat for the first time in Ukraine last fall infuriated Russian officials.

Mr. Erdogan's decision to provide weapons and diplomatically back Ukraine was a public rebuke to Moscow and another complicating factor in the mix of cooperation and conflict between Turkey and Russia, historical rivals for supremacy in the region around the Black Sea.

The promise of more arms for Ukraine, especially an offensive weapon like the Bayraktar TB-2 Turkish drone, is an extremely sensitive issue for Moscow, which claims that its security is threatened.

An American airlift of anti-tank missiles and small-arms ammunition continued with the arrival of a seventh cargo jet of weaponry to Kyiv.

At the same time, Russia denounced the Biden administration's announcement that it would send additional troops to NATO countries, with the Kremlin spokesman, Dmitri S. Peskov, accusing the United States of "igniting tensions on the European continent."

Russia's defense minister, Sergei K. Shoigu, said that the Russian military would send additional troops and equipment for military exercises in Belarus, which borders Ukraine to the north, adding to tens of thousands of soldiers already deployed there.

Turkey is a member of NATO but also maintains economic and military industry ties with Russia. And the two countries are also on opposing sides in two Middle Eastern wars, in Syria and Libya, and in the conflict between Azerbaijan and Armenia in the South Caucasus region.

Turkey has sold Ukraine armed Bayraktar TB2 drones that the Ukrainian military used for the first time in combat in the war with Russian-backed separatists last October.

Earlier, in a bid to reassure Moscow, the Turkish defense minister, Hulusi Akar, stressed Ankara's commitment to a treaty that restricts NATO forces' access to the Black Sea through the Bosporus and Dardanelles Straits, which Turkey controls. The accord, 'the Montreux Convention', prohibits aircraft carriers from crossing the straits and limits other warships to short voyages in the Black Sea.

Seven American cargo jets have carried a total of about 600 tons of military assistance so far including anti-tank weapons and small-arms ammunition.

The shipments included additional Javelin anti-tank missiles from the United States. Britain has airlifted about 2,000 light anti-tank missiles, known as NLAWs, to Ukraine in the past two weeks.

With approval from the United States, the Baltic countries of

Estonia, Latvia and Lithuania said they would transfer more Javelin anti-tank missiles and Stinger antiaircraft missiles, plugging some holes in Ukraine's air defenses. Poland has also said it will send antiaircraft missiles.

With the additional British and American supplies, Ukraine now has more anti-tank missiles than Russia has operational main battle tanks in its military, though Russia's total including tanks in reserve is still larger.

Ukraine does not have to reach a so-called 'capability parity' with the Russian Army — an impossibility in any case — to deter a military intervention.

Towards World War III

We drive back from the base at Geçitkale to our apartments in Limassol. It already feels as if we have been here a month, although I realise it is only a matter of days. Human time can be dense.

Christina has phoned ahead and explained to the others that everything had gone to plan. I notice she speaks in a semi-coded way to the others and realise she is still thinking about us being bugged.

Back in our rooms, Charlie calls a meeting for us to plan the next steps. Antanov is concerned about the Tupolev being discovered and we are all worried about what we'd unleash if we activated the drones.

It will be our third night in Limassol and we all think will need to move the next day. We rebalance the occupants of the apartments so that Christina and Antanov, and Irina and Eckhart can share rooms.

That evening we sit on Christina's balcony discussing options.

"We've little choice but to start something if we genuinely want to end this war. However, if Putin has really activated the Perimeter system, then there could be nothing left at the end of it," says Charlie.

"I think there's often a coup to finish this kind of tyrant," says Christina.

Antanov adds, "Think about it: In most cases, scenarios of future war have rarely come to pass as originally envisioned. At least two inter-related reasons can account for this.

"First, due to the incredibly large number of variables to consider – geopolitical, technical, human, etc. – it is simply impossible to calculate how they will interact with each other"

"Yes," agrees Christina, "The second reason has to do with distinguishing between 'future war' and the 'future battlefield.' Regrettably, too many scenarios and models, whether developed by military organisations, political scientists, or fiction writers, tend to focus their attention on the battlefield and the clash of armies, navies, air forces, and especially their weapons systems."

Antanov agrees, "You are right. The broader context of the war needs to be examined – the reasons why hostilities erupted, the political and military objectives, the limits placed on military action, and so on. They are given much less serious attention, often because they are viewed as a distraction from the main activity that occurs on the battlefield."

Eckhart joins in, "Putin's decision for war initiation is almost superficial. Most wars have a run-rate of costs, and the Americans usually factor that into their economic calculations.

"Yes, but those calculations are also off by billions of dollars," said Antanov, "And then the contractors brought in to tidy up are onto a huge money-making scheme. Halliburton, Kellogg, Brown and Root and Bechtel along with Brant Industry and others, have made huge contracts in countries that had been demolished."

Eckhart continues, "Putin's decision to attack Ukraine is not one based on a Kremlin desire for world conquest, but rather as a defensive move motivated by fears of the elite. The fears that the future 'correlation of forces' won't favour the Kremlin and that internal weakness will lead to state collapse. Putin wants to re-establish boundaries but with one less variable. He can't stand the thought of Ukraine becoming friendly with NATO."

Antanov adds, "Then there's the timing of the war initiation. It hardly came as a surprise, with all the protracted build-up of troops close to the Ukrainian and Belorussian borders. Of course, the whole build-up was covered in lies, which the west was only too grateful to believe. Putin on the other hand would say anything he could get away with.

Christina adds, "He messed up the war logistics though. Frightened soldiers under the reign of Dedovshchina and kept in the dark about their mission. Faulty main battle tanks with insufficient fuel and armaments that can't withstand modern weapons like the American Javelin and Anglo-Swedish Next-generation Light Anti-Tank Weapons (NLAWs). Planes that could hardly fly and weapons systems that were unreliable. Shoigu must have been mad to agree to start hostilities in that condition."

Eckhart adds, "Then there's the boundary conditions of the onslaught. Ukraine now, but Moldova and Latvia next? I'm sure the war planners have looked into both scenarios."

Christina adds, "More fundamental is whether Putin expects to cross the nuclear threshold. On the NATO side, Supreme Allied Commander Europe and Supreme Allied Commander Atlantic could be pressed to authorise the use of tactical nuclear weapons against Soviet ground and naval forces. In war games they always refuse, fearing a Kremlin escalation. On the Kremlin side, there's little in the path of a determined Putin and even less in the way should Perimeter be triggered."

Antanov continues, "If Putin really doesn't care, and his military losses suggest he doesn't, then I'd expect to see chemical weapons deployed next. We'll see"

Antanov adds, "Writing an ending to a third world war is as difficult as writing the beginning. In the scenarios discussed here, unlike in much of the nuclear fiction genre, the war does not end in global Armageddon. I predict that the war will end with a coup in the Kremlin, or wherever the main controllers of the war sit. One feature that is pretty much a constant in all these scenarios is that as the war is taking place, so too are diplomatic negotiations. The problem is that the man on one side of the equation is a proven liar and may just be stalling for time to reposition or refresh their troops."

Charlie interrupts, "That's just it. We need to hasten the coup. Make Putin's supporters very afraid of the consequences."

I once again wonder why - as Watchers - none of the three of us can remember anything about the Klima Wars, nor how they start.

PART THREE

Eve of Destruction

The Eastern world, it is explodin'
  Violence flarin', bullets loadin'
  You're old enough to kill but not for votin'
  You don't believe in war, but what's that gun you're totin'?
  And even the Jordan river has bodies floatin'

But you tell me
  Over and over and over again, my friend
  How you don't believe
  We're on the eve of destruction

Don't you understand what I'm trying to say
  Can't you feel the fears I'm feeling today?
  If the button is pushed, there's no runnin' away
  There'll be no one to save with the world in a grave
  Take a look around you boy, it's bound to scare you, boy

And you tell me
  Over and over and over again, my friend
  How you don't believe
  We're on the eve of destruction

Yeah, my blood's so mad, feels like coagulatin'
  I'm sittin' here just contemplatin'
  I can't twist the truth, it knows no regulation
  Handful of senators don't pass legislation
  And marches alone can't bring integration
  When human respect is disintegratin'
  This whole crazy world is just too frustratin'

And you tell me
  Over and over and over and over again, my friend
  You don't believe we're on the eve of destruction
  No no, you don't believe we're on the eve of destruction

Phil Sloan / Steve Barri

How to create Rage

"We'll need to create a rage in the Kremlin. Instead of pointing outwards, it will need to be internal," says Christina.

"Financial first?" suggests Charlie, "If all those Kremlin elite think they are going to lose their wealth..."

"Maybe we should add some property damage to the equation?" suggests Chantal, "Imagine if a stack of drones deployed themselves over Krasnodar Krai?"

"And perhaps that Tupolev can be rediscovered on a course for Moscow?" adds Antonov.

"We need to get ahead of the Perimeter system, somehow," Eckhart adds, "If *Mertvaya Ruka* - Dead Hand - gets actioned, then an ageing Soviet command missile will fly right across Russia triggering all of the nuclear silos."

"That sounds like enough," says Christina.

"Enough for what?" I ask.

Christina spoke, "Enough to bring forward whatever plan the Kremlin elite have created to depose Putin. Vitalievich can't have been the only one with plans. Their rage is heightened since we now know that both the siloviki and the liberals are already arguing in the Kremlin, but that everyone is living in an information famine. It is destroying the Motherland."

Antonov speaks, "That plane we borrowed, it is a Tu-160M1 with the new navigation system and ABSU-200 autopilot. We can set it on its way, parachute out and let it continue crewless. I suggest we set its course for either Putin's Palace or the underground bunker."

"The threat is only good if they know the plane contains 4 nuclear warheads," says Christina.

Antonov answers, "That's easy to arrange. I'll light it up for the piloted part and then go stealth for the second part of the journey, but with a clear vector."

"But won't you have to fly slow for the parachute exit?" I ask.

"Correct, I'll pre-program the flight to pick up speed after we are clear. Think of it as fire and forget," answers Antanov, "Hey, Christina and I have done this over the White Sea about a dozen times."

"Never in a supersonic bomber though," says Christina.

Charlie and I exchange a look.

"You know something," I say, "I think I should fly the Tupolev. Maybe with Charlie?"

Antanov looks surprised, "Why? Do you have experience

with this kind of plane?"

"Yes, I've flown thousands of air miles in dozens of different planes. I had to pilot a stolen Sukhoi-27 to get out of Ukraine on the way here. It also had a glass cockpit, so I'm used to them. In my head I keep thinking of a X-Blade plane too. Not something from the movies, but something futuristic that I think Scrive has flown before, with modifications applied to it by Charlie."

It's very strange at this moment, answering as Farallon via Scrive's Presence - and even weirder having 'jamais vu'/ 'flash-forward' moments, yet not being able to recall Big History.

"My main thought is that even if I do it, it is impossible for me to be in direct jeopardy, and neither can Charlie. If something happens to us, we will be placed back on the timeline in our own metaverse, I guess we will be close to our friend Drake. I know, it sounds like we've been eating the magic mushrooms, but it is true."

Charlie adds, "Scrive is right. If you, Antanov, or you, Christina, get into trouble, you will find yourselves back on the almost parallel path in your own metaverse. The same goes for Irina and Eckhart."

"Leaving just me!" says Chantal, "But you know something? I can create quite a lot of chaos now I know this version of reality is expendable."

She continues, "As an example, I can create some new news. Imagine if the western press started to publish cover stories in Russian. We could set a cat amongst the pigeons!

Chantal looks gleeful, "I've already suggested it to a

leading western left-leaning tabloid in London. If the Daily Mirror goes large with something aimed at the Russian people, then it can only be a matter of time before a few copycat articles appear. They won't be able to hold back every news item unless they entirely shut Russia off from the world."

"And most of the Russian elite also speak English as well," says Charlie, "It will be quite unsettling."

"Not as unsettling as having your hometown bombed to extinction by Russian militia," says Chantal.

Russian Laundry

Chantal continues, "I think we can also up the economic stakes further. I know that Scrive and Charlie spent a lot of time in London, England. Well, so did I. I even had to work in one of those investment houses. I know that over the past two decades, London became one of the preferred investment locations for Russian oligarchs, as well a key financial centre for Russian companies, all encouraged by British governments.

"London was known as 'the laundromat': an apparatus that allowed billions of pounds — some of it obtained through illegal or questionable means — to be siphoned out of the Russian economy and into trophy assets in the UK.

"Then, to cement things, people started to call London 'Londongrad'."

I knew this, of course, but wondered what Chantal was planning.

"We can use the strength to become a weakness," she explains, "The first wave of Russians to invest in UK real estate was new money wanting very substantial properties. The properties on the wish list were the biggest and the best, including some very close to the monarch's property in Buckingham Palace."

Chantal continues, "This is how we - I - can exploit the situation. The lack of UK rules requiring full disclosure of foreign owners of British property was an attraction for the Russian super-rich, who appreciated the privacy. If you came along with a photocopy of your passport, that was enough to be deemed suitable.

"Then, Transparency International, the anti-corruption campaign group, identified £-billions of UK property — nearly 150 land titles — bought by Russians who have been accused of links to the Kremlin or corruption. That is where we can strike."

Chantal asks, "Do you see? Under -regulated acquisitions held anonymously, but with a list available from Transparency International? We can tilt the table. Make all of the balls run our way."

Chantal adds, "Transparency International UK has been collating information on questionable funds from around the world being invested in UK property since 2016. This figure now stands at £6.7 billion. Of this total, £1.5 billion worth of property was bought by Russians accused of corruption or links to the Kremlin. Nearly £430 million worth is in the City of Westminster, while £283 million is in Kensington and Chelsea. Their analysis of how this £1.5 billion is owned reveals over half is held by companies in Britain's Overseas Territories and Crown Dependencies. The secrecy provided by these offshore financial centres is often used by those seeking to hide their ownership of assets.

"Then, they identified over two thousand companies

registered in the UK and its Overseas Territories and Crown Dependencies used in around 50 Russian money laundering and corruption cases. These cases involved more than £80 billion worth of funds diverted by rigged procurement, bribery, embezzlement and the unlawful acquisition of state assets."

Chantal pauses, then adds, "If I start looking at the Transparency lists, I can arrange for most of the assets to progressively drift toward a single, newly minted entity."

"The oligarchs will be furious!" says Christina, "But to do it you'd have to do several large-scale illegal things."

"Welcome to my world of chaos," says Chantal, "It's why we can act but the world can't."

"I knew that some of Putin's inner circle used to favour those Caribbean regions - sometimes they would be arriving to meet Putin or leaving to go on a visit to the islands," says Antanov.

Chantal adds, "Yes, that is why so many banks have Caribbean desks, often specialising in the British Virgin Islands - usually called BVI. In fact, the most vocal resistance to beneficial ownership transparency has come from the British Virgin Islands. The Transparency International research highlighted how criminals favoured BVI companies as money laundering vehicles, with over 90 per cent - that's over 1000 - of the legal entities used in over 200 major corruption and money laundering cases incorporated in this jurisdiction. Their use by people smuggling illicit loot across borders is so prolific that 'BVI' risks becoming synonymous with questionable financial dealings."

She adds, "To give an idea of the depth of criminality, the BVI's special envoy may seek to renegotiate its constitutional relationship with the UK to avoid having to implement public beneficial ownership registers. Part of the BVI's reticence to introduce transparency is the perception that this would drive business from its shores, which would have severe consequences for its public finances. According to its latest budget estimates, receipts from its corporate register – the biggest by far in the UK's offshore financial centres – account for almost 60 per cent of its state revenue."

"This looks like an interesting place to drop some chaos," said Christina.

"Well, it looks as if it has already started," said Chantal, "UK Prime Minister Boris Johnson declared he wants to impose punitive sanctions on individuals and companies with links to the Kremlin as well as crack down on money laundering."

"But it's probably not true?" asks Antanov, "I mean, that man has too many links to Russia and aren't his cabinet so many puppets of the Kremlin?"

Charlie speaks, "Yes, despite the bold rhetoric, it is not clear the laggardly Johnson government has either the political will or the tools to completely strip illicit money from the UK financial system. And there would be too many senior fat cats embarrassed if their sources of funding dried up. Once more I sense hollow words."

Chantal says, "We can also get the 2020 report by the UK parliament's intelligence and security committee. It noted that several British politicians had business interests linked to Russia or worked directly for major companies with ties to the Russian state. The report also highlighted a supporting cast of advisers, including bankers, lawyers, and estate agents, who were on hand to provide their services to oligarchs and Russian companies. It said that Russian money had been used in extending patronage and building influence across a wide sphere of the British establishment — public relations firms, charities, political interests, academia, and cultural institutions were all willing beneficiaries of Russian money. The report found that certain members of the Russian elite who were closely linked to Putin had donated to UK political parties and had a public profile which positions them to assist Russian influence operations.

Charlie says, "Go Chantal! go Limantour! It looks as if you have identified a whole house of cards which we could assist to tumble."

"But if we can do it, then why can't the prevailing legislation?" asks Eckhart.

Chantal says, "It's the art of managing the long grass. Any scoundrel will kick anything controversial into the long grass. They can just say that successive governments have faced a consistent problem: how to distinguish between the Russians whose money has been made in a legitimate manner, and the crooked others. Take 2018, when the May government introduced a measure called unexplained wealth orders. When certain criteria are met, they require the owner of an asset worth more than £50,000 to explain how they could afford it. But, so far, only a handful of orders have been issued by the courts.

"It's all very well now to say UK is no place for dirty money, no more golden visas awarded to overseas millionaires, increased placing of sanctions, but everything moves so slowly."

"Like partygate?" asks Irina, "You know, where some illegal parties were held in 10 Downing Street?"

Christina nods, "Just like partygate. They took too long and issued too few warrants; the fines were often for a derisory amount. The whole issue of repeated lies to parliament was deftly side-stepped. These people know how to dodge just about everything."

"Well, we'll see about that," smiles Chantal.

Charlie's plan.

Charlie stands and walks around the balcony. We still had beautiful views of the green sea and sky. I was even getting used to the unusual colours.

"Let's recap," Charlie says,

"We can fly a stealth bomber towards Putin's bunker.

"We can set off some drones, from Turkish Cyprus, targeted on the Ozero commune.

"We can run confusion through their information channels

"We can disrupt the financial system, which will massively inconvenience the oligarchs.

"But we need someone else to be triggered to action too," says Christina.

"Don't you think this is enough?" asks Chantal, "Will the Kremlin elite, who must be plotting some kind of coup, be triggered into action when they see how bad things can turn for Russia?"

Irina speaks, "We must tell Blackbird about the HVAC at the Altai bunker. That the air-con is part of the bunker defences."

"Putin's enemies will be planning to use some form of OTC," answers Eckhart. "It is the most reliably available nerve agent in Russia."

"Organophosphate Toxic Chemicals?" queries Charlie, "But I thought they were made illegal many years ago?"

"They were," answers Eckart, "but it is no secret that disposal is expensive. Nor is it a secret that the Russian Biopreparat program identified more lethal airborne toxins than even the American VX toxin."

"Eckhart is correct," says Irina, "So far, it is not clear how to get rid of residues of toxic chemicals and toxic products because of their impact in the environment.

Irina adds, "The army does not know, because it did not deal with questions of decontamination of civilian facilities that were not involved in military operations, and army requirements for results of decontamination are many orders of magnitude less stringent. Nor has civilian 'applied science' worked out these methods and standards, because in the early eighties it was only planning to organize such research at Novocheboksarsk."

She continues, "We saw these plans die along with the elimination of the laboratory. With the fall of the Soviet Union, Soviet properties were scrapped or deserted, along with their missions. It wasn't just Putin burning records. There has been practically no organisation of special ecological monitoring around today's chemical weapons storage bases, even though chemical weapons will have to stay there for a very long time."

Eckart continues, "Irina is right, The Convention on Chemical Disarmament has so far not only been unfulfilled by Russia but has actually been violated through the theatrical open destruction of chemical weapons. The Russian answer to ceasing production of the weapons was to build stores for them instead. The original organophosphorus toxins produced paralytic nerve action: tabun (GA), sarin (GB), soman (GD) and V-gases. The first three toxins were developed in Germany at the turn of the nineteen-forties and are usually referred to as second generation nerve agents."

He adds, "Third generation agents were developed during the Foliant program and yielded five toxins of a new type. One of these was refined into a fourth-generation nerve agent (A-232, "novichok-5"). This turned out to be convenient for combat use and could be stored in a in binary form.

I realised that the binary storage meant it is not breaking any conventions. Only when they get combined do the separate agents become lethal.

"Okay, my revised recap," says Charlie.

"We can fly a stealth bomber towards Putin's bunker.

"We can set off some drones, from Turkish Cyprus, targeted on the Ozero commune.

"We can disrupt the financial system, to inconvenience the oligarchs by stealing their money.

"We can let Putin's elite enemies know about the weakness of the Altai complex, via Blackbird.

"And the information chaos is already running."

"Right, let's get moving," says Antanov.

Ride a white swan

Ride it on out like a bird in the sky ways
Ride it on out like you were a bird
Fly it all out like an eagle in a sunbeam
Ride it on out like you were a bird

Wear a tall hat like a druid in the old days
Wear a tall hat and a tattooed gown
Ride a white swan like the people of the Beltane
Wear your hair long, babe you can't go wrong

Catch a bright star and a place it on your forehead
Say a few spells and baby, there you go
Take a black cat and sit it on your shoulder
And in the morning, you'll know all you know, oh

Marc Bolan

If the money's no good

Chantal speaks up, "I've been looking at how we can move some of that money around. We should chaotically disrupt a few things. Their way to move funds was a repeating pattern. All the oligarch core-group companies appeared to be owned by proxies standing in for hidden owners. Even directors and shareholders of the companies were fake.

"Some payments did go to genuine companies for real goods – but the transactions were made not by their clients, but by 21 core companies using bogus copy-pasted paperwork which specified goods the company didn't sell.

"Some payments went to another layer of shell companies, like the core group making the payments from Trasta Komercbanka, in Riga, Latvia.

"But isn't this how all Russian clients do business?" asked Christina.

"Not exactly," answers Chantal, "Heavy users of the scheme were rich and powerful Russians who had made their fortunes. After all the middle moves, payments of laundered money slid easily into the world's biggest international banks."

I consider how this Laundromat illustrates that the world's banking system has been impotent, unable to staunch massive flows of illicit money. Bank officials offer several reasons as to why this is so – including that their Russian counterparts have not been helpful.

I recollect that HSBC, Deutsche Bank, Bank of China, Bank of America, Danske Bank, and Emirates NBD Bank all ended up with tainted money.

FSB representatives served on the board of at least one of banks that wired billions out of Russia as did Igor Putin, Putin's cousin. He was a manager and executive board member in the Russian Land Bank. This bank wired more than $9.7 billion to Moldindconbank in Moldova, most of which went on to Trasta Komercbanka and from there on to the world.

"Now that is an interesting pinch point," said Christina.

Chantal nodded, "Yes, if we can connect a fake BVI corporation to Russian Land Bank's outbound correspondent banks, we will have a way to siphon off large amounts of Russian money. We can place it in the new account and there it will be almost impossible to trace."

She smiled, "Of course, I'd have to do something illegal to make such a scheme viable,"

"What?" asked Antanov, intrigued.

"Just add a little something; something chaotic!" answered Chantal," I can just slightly tilt the way that Russia perceives itself.

She smiled, "We can also export chaos through information management. Like the earlier Project Russia papers, we can produce something new, and distribute it by the same method. It will look as if the FSB have engineered something. In this case, we can ensure that Russia and the west get access."

She continues, "The storyline needs to be about foreign companies leaving Russia. We can signal in our document that the departures are a torrent and of the unintended consequences for average citizens.

"When you think about a business, you think about the owners of the capital and the owners of the labour. A lot of these companies have employees in Russia, and these departures also directly affect the Russian people."

"But won't the Russian people be indoctrinated with the Russian line that everyone in the west is writing propaganda to fool them?" asks Charlie.

Chantal answers, "I agree, that can happen, but we are not so much targeting the average Russian, as we are targeting the oligarchs and elite. The people who are already inside the circle and can see what is really happening. This will reinforce their views. I think we may need a news source to uncharacteristically publish something in Russian to help spread the word."

Chantal continues to speak, "We don't even need to fabricate much. Think about it. On February 24th, Russia launched a full-scale military attack on Ukraine, and faced a wall of global outrage. Three days later, BP announced that it was abandoning its stake in the Russian oil giant Rosneft, at a cost to the company of up to twenty-five billion dollars. The next day, Shell announced that it was leaving, too, withdrawing from a partnership with Gazprom and the Nord Stream 2 natural-gas pipeline. Then Germany revoked its interest in Nord Stream 2. Alone those few moves will have crippled the Russian equity holdings in those companies.

"The following day, Exxon announced that it would leave as well. Shell's C.E.O. seemed to speak for more than just himself when he said he was shocked by the deplorable loss of life in Ukraine resulting from a senseless act of military aggression which threatens European security.

Christina agrees, "We need to lay it out for the elite of Russia. The fossil-fuel giants lobbed some of the earliest salvos in what has since amounted to a private-sector declaration of war on Russia, which has now seen an astonishing four hundred and fifty companies announce a withdrawal, suspension, or scaling back of business in Russia.

She gestured towards her laptop, "Look, I've found this list of business departures from Russia. After the oil giants, the next big surprise was the speed which major consulting firms such as Bain & Company, Boston Consulting Group, and McKinsey & Company, decided to pull out.

"They would usually rather jump off a cliff than get involved in political conflict or geopolitics. They were followed by the major accounting firms, and a long list of global law firms.

"And then you had big tech companies. Dell, I.B.M., Apple, HP, Google, Meta, and Twitter suspended some or all operations in Russia."

Christina interrupts, "Yes, I can see where this is going. A report could crystallise such a situation for the Kremlin elite. We will need to make a few basic statements. The kind which would get a source arrested. Except we will be using the same tricks that the FSB did to launch Project Russia. That includes anonymity. Our report can say that the global business exodus from Russia serves as a powerful condemnation of Russian President Vladimir Putin.

"It will also underscore that his military invasion of Ukraine is not only going to devastate that country but will also cripple the Russian Motherland."

Yarost

"We'll need to set the Tupolev back on a course, maybe to Putin's Palace. We could remodel the Black Sea with its payload," said Charlie, "Although we don't think we'll have to use it, will we?"

"Correct, " I say, "We need them to think we could use it. That should be enough."

"But will they try to shoot us down?" asks Charlie.

"Unlikely," answers Antanov, "They will want to persuade you to surrender and then bring the plane down without any explosions. But they will be worried that you could activate one of those warheads. And, think about it, you'll be flying a Russian plane in Russia."

Christina adds, "It will be at the same time as a squadron of drones are flying to the dachas of Putin's elite. They will not like it."

"Well, I wondered if those co-ordinates would come in useful," says Antanov, "Remember, when we were at the Ozero. I saved the GPS for each of the properties. Now we have some useful drones to point at them. This is going to take a convincing phone call from Tümgeneral Nott to the base commander at Geçitkale. She even left them with a secret trigger code word. Ярост -Yarost'"

"It means 'Rage'."

"I will speak to them in English - except for the code word," says Christina, "And we had better make it urgent, so that they don't have time to query things. I'm sure they will love to send a whole flight of their Bayraktars skyward,"

"But will they have enough range?" asks Charlie.

"Sure," says Antanov, "Those things have a 6000 km range at an altitude of up to 8 kilometres.

Christina adds, "But they are quite slow, only 200 km per hour."

Antanov speaks, "It's about 3,100 kilometres to Leshkovo from Cyprus, so that would take around 16 hours at the drone's cruising speed. We can certainly introduce some chaos."

Chantal had been studying the financial systems and scribbling onto a small black notepad.

"It's been slightly difficult, but I've found several transactions which will help us plug into their money transfer system," she explained, "The transactions have been listed for other reasons, usually because they are exhibits in a court case but didn't get redacted."

"Because I know I'm looking for a certain Russian Bank, it means I can filter down the accounts to a few suspects. Then I can rewire routing to come into our account instead of the originally intended one. It is total fraud and theft but is the fastest way to shut down the money laundering. I'm also attacking the bulk endpoint of these transactions. Where it will really hurt."

Irina asks, "But wait a minute, if you can do this, then why can't anyone else? Maybe a government, or even a bank wanting to stay legal?"

"It's because I'm prepared to break the law spectacularly to achieve this," explained Chantal. "Any government would have to go through so much legislation to get to this point, and any bank would have lawyers crawling all over such a process. Don't forget, the people doing these things want time to react. I'm just closing that door."

"Is that why it took so long for initial sanctions to be imposed?" asked Charlie, "It seemed to take weeks?"

"Exactly," answered Chantal, "It's also heavily political."

Christina nodded her agreement, "It's a KGB Rulebook 101 - and I do mean KGB -it has been around for so long. None of these kleptocrats want anything to be too speedy. They want time to move their money, their yachts, mistresses, families, and their planes. A large part of the financial and legal infrastructure in certain countries revolves around assisting these criminals."

"It was interesting when that UK report came out in 2019," said Antanov, "The so-called Russia Report. That buffoon of a UK Prime Minister tried to suppress it whilst the Kremlin was laughing at the name Londongrad given to London."

Eckhart speaks, "If the kleptocrats think they can sit out these latest sanctions, then they will. Their model is to steal money leveraged by the Russian state and then to offshore it, paying a fealty to the Kremlin. But fall behind with payments and you'll be likely to receive a plutonium sandwich."

"It's why I'm moving the money to a hedge fund," said Chantal. "Партнеры треугольника

Partnery treugol'nika" - Triangle Associates. It will be impossible to find anything when I've finished, just a huge ball of interlinked nominees and directors. Only we will have access to the available funds, but no-one else. Look, I can set up multiple companies in minutes for payments of £12 per company. And I'll never have to pay any tax, because I'll have them all showing a loss and closed inside of a year."

"I like your choice of name, Christina, by the way, it's very much in the mould of other funds like: Blackrock Advisors, Bridgewater Associates, Renaissance Technologies, Two Sigma Investments, Millennium Management, Citadel Advisors. You'd hardly know that, for example, Citadel started out of a 19-year-old's dorm room in 1987 trading convertible bonds.

"But what about us? Asked Christina.

"Oh no, we have a thoroughly respectable back story and a wonderful web site. I've just scraped a competitor and chaotically renamed everything. I can't fake the comparison ratings though, but there are plenty of other funds that show as unrated."

Chantal continues, "Hedge Funds are still an instrument of choice when involved with this class of fraud. Christina picks a Glock, and I pick a Hedge Fund. They can both do serious damage. Hedge Funds can suppress pro-social behaviour, which is ideally suited to the lifestyle of a kleptocrat. It is a case of the strength becoming a weakness. They already have dead social consciences, now there is a worrying personal impact as well."

Christina laughs, "SIG Sauer, actually,"

Chantel continues and lists: "Example 1: Authority Doesn't Care About Ethics. Since the days of Stanley Milgram's notorious electric shock experiments, behavioural science has shown that people do what they are instructed to do. Hedge fund traders are routinely instructed by their managers and investors to focus on maximising portfolio returns. Thus, it should come as no surprise that not all hedge fund traders put obeying federal securities laws at the top of their to-do lists.

"Example 2: Other Traders Aren't Acting Ethically. Behavioural experiments also routinely find that people are most likely to 'follow their conscience' when they think others are also acting pro-socially. Yet in the hedge fund environment, traders are more likely to brag about their superior results than their willingness to sacrifice those results to preserve their ethics.

"Example 3: Unethical Behaviour Isn't Harmful. Finally, experiments show that people act less selfishly when they understand how their selfishness harms others. This poses special problems for enforcing laws against insider trading, which is often perceived as a 'victimless' crime that may even contribute to social welfare by producing more accurate market prices. Of course, insider trading isn't victimless: for every trader who reaps a gain using insider information, some investor on the other side of the trade must lose. But because the losing investor is distant and anonymous, it's easy to mistakenly feel that insider trading isn't really doing harm.

Chantal continues, "I just need to mimic the behaviour of other bad apple traders and we should soon have turned off all of the funding taps to those oligarchs. They will not be pleased but won't know where their money has gone."

The mistress of chaos smiles at me. Limantour was enjoying this.

Eckhart speaks, "I just heard from Sorokoput - Irina's and my handler. It is very dangerous, because although I think Christina and Eckhart's handler Blackbird is damaged goods, Sorokoput maybe playing both ends against the middle."

Chantal asks, "Do you think you can trust him?"

"Irina speaks, "Her, actually. Sorokoput - butcher bird - is a woman. I never have really trusted her, but now I guess she can see the writing on the wall."

Eckhart speaks again, "Well, Sorokoput says that Altai have just received a consignment of nerve agent. It was ordered by the President."

Chantal asks, "But where would they get it from?"

Antanov speaks, "Indeed, but you have to remember Russia once held 40,000 metric tons of chemical weapons and then very slowly started to dispose of them.

"My guess is the last nerve agent store house or maybe the last couple have remained in use. It would also explain where The Kremlin could get novichok and other nerve agents used in various assassinations and assassination attempts. Think about it: Yuschenko, Navalny, Litvinenko, Skripal, Abramovich...the list goes on."

Eckhart speaks again, "This sounds like a whole truck load of dangerous chemicals has been shipped to the Altai bunker, from Shikany-2."

Antanov speaks, "Shikany-2 is a military town. I was continuously scared when I was posted there for a couple of weeks. I had to run security for a couple of young scientists named Panyaev and Kudryavtsev who worked for FSB's Criminalistics Institute – also known as its poisons factory. They had a special project, but I was pulled out before it ran to conclusion. I think they were deliberately moving us around so that no-one knew the big picture. The town itself was a closed town. No-one allowed in unless they had a strong reason."

Antanov adds, "Shikany-2 is close to the Volga and about 100 kilometres north-east of Saratov. It used to have a code name Tomko. The Shikany-2 facility includes a chemical weapons burial site with approximately 4,000 metric tons of adamsite - That's the riot control agent that causes vomiting - and the adamsite was collected from all over the former Soviet Union."

Antanov continues, "Shikany-2 was where Col Stanislav Makshakov, a top-notch military scientist was based. He worked at the State Organic Synthesis Institute. Makshakov used to report to Gen Kirill Vasilyev, director of the FSB Criminalistics Institute. Vasilyev then reported to Maj Gen Vladimir Bogdanov, former chief of the Criminalistics Institute and deputy director of the FSB's Scientific-Technical Service. Vasilyev's direct superior is the FSB's director Alexander Bortnikov. He still, in turn, reports to Putin."

Christina adds, "Okay, so now we are seeing a truckload of one of their products being shipped to Putin's bunker? This can only end badly."

"Assuming that Sorokoput is telling the truth."

"You know something, her knowledge of that is probably the reason why she is suddenly open.

"Do we know whether Putin ordered it? Or someone else?"

"No, we don't, but either way, it helps our case."

A hard rain is gonna fall.

Charlie summarised "Okay, so now we have the pieces in place.

"We can send the stealth bomber to Putin's Palace
"We can target the drones on the Ozero Community
"We can stop the entire money flows of the kleptocrats
"We can disrupt the security of the Altai base.

If some of these conditions happen, I think we will see a change from the oligarchs. The elites will realise that this too much. That the situation is out of control.

And it is not obvious where the impacts have come from either. It won't look as if America or the United Nations has intervened.

"We will have chaos," says Chantal gleefully, "That's when things could change suddenly."

"We three, Scrive, Charlie and me; we have a way to get back into the correct timeline and metaverse. I should hitch a ride with Scrive and Charlie. They can show me how to be the flight engineer.

"The rest of you, Christina, Antanov, Eckhart and Irina,

will be switched back into your original times and places. You will be safe, but much of what has happened here may need to play out again. I doubt you will remember much, but it will feel instinctive to each of you to take certain actions."

"I wish we could tell you how this ends," said Charlie, "But none of us have recall of these events. But when we are back on our correct lines we will know. Like we will all remember about the Klima Wars and how they started."

We all stood and looked at one another. I was aware that the sky was an even deeper green than normal, and the sea reflected the colour.

Chantal put her hand into the middle of us group in a circle. We all did the same.

"Slava Ukraini", she said. We all repeated it and then hugged one another. And again a second hug.

"At least, in this metaverse," Chantal added.

"Okay," said Christina, "Let's hit it, then."

Chantal and Christina make busy with the phones. Chantal shows us the capital in the new Triangle Associates Hedge Fund. It is already over half a billion dollars. That's in a few hours. And I think that it is half a billion dollars that is not with the Kremlin elite. I sense a few fuses blowing.

Christina has been onto the Bayraktar base and has now sent a dozen drones toward their GPS co-ordinates.

She speaks, "I added Putin's Palace as well, and the

Kremlin for good luck. Those last two will be shot down, but it shows our intent. The hard rain is gonna fall,' "

I was thinking, 'Yes, rain from 8 kilometres high'.

Antanov called Artem, and in ten minutes he was outside to take me, Chantal, and Charlie back to RAF Akrotiri. We say good-bye to him at the base, and he says he'll look forward to seeing us the next time. I wonder what he means.

Now, we are both back in green flight suits looking at the Tupolev, which has been moved into a hangar. I can understand why its nickname is The White Swan.

We climb in for what we realise will be the last time. Almost the last time in this version of Earth.

We are about to start up when Charlie says something.

"Remember our original intervention? When we used your gravity wave to trigger another event? - We talked then about unexpected consequences?"

I remembered, even although the last part of what had happened seemed to have been erased.

"Well, you, Farallon, haven't been using your gravity power much since we arrived here."

I wasn't sure where this was leading. Did she want me to levitate the plane or something?"

"I've some co-ordinates here,' She pulls open her zipper pocket and pulled out a folded sheet of A4. On it were some GPS numbers.

50.78129882, 86.48117964

"These are Putin's bunker co-ordinates. Remember it is full of tunnels and may now be storing some unstable chemical from a poison lab?"

I realised what she was asking.

"I guess you could shake things up a little around there. Maybe a new hole in the ground. The river Katun could find a new path and it could all be mixed up with some of that chemical?"

"But it would be another Intervention," I say.

"Yes, but look where we are. This is like the last reel of a movie, or the last few pages of a novel. We know that there must be another way. We are just trying to force it."

I look at Charlie.

"Oh, okay, give me the co-ords."

I knew I'd need to concentrate, and that I could either fly the plane or do some kind of gravity shift.

The weak force won. We watched as the sky rippled.

"Thank you," said Charlie,

The headphones crackled: 'Line up and wait'; 'Cleared for runway two seven '; 'Fly heading two three zero,' 'Runway two seven, Cleared for take-off,' then he added 'Godspeed'.

Our Tupolev sped forward. We'd be climbing to an obscene altitude and flying at a crazy speed pulling a sonic boom in our wake.

It didn't matter if this variant of Earth was ready to implode.

I looked first at Charlie and then behind me to Chantal. They were both smiling. We'd set so many hares running now. The Bayraktars. The diverted oligarch money. Misinformation. A natural catastrophe at Putin's bunker, with toxins blended with river water. Maybe a crazy man's Perimeter system, triggering the Dead Hand. We would never know.

It was no longer 'If', just 'When'.

"Look!" said Charlie. I almost hadn't noticed. We were at 40,000 feet, still climbing. The sky had changed. No longer green, it was restored to blue.

A judder.

"See you both on the other side!" called Charlie.

Rage

Farallon and Limantour

Another judder.

He heard the apartment judder from the impact. A mournful sigh. This one had been close, but not that close. He knew the building was meant to take it.

He looked towards the window. Grey night skies, something resembling clouds, thin trails, raked towards the horizon.

It had happened, he was someone new. He thought he'd have been restarted close to the spot where everything and become chaotic, courtesy of Chantal. Now he looked at the clock. Ten minutes to midnight.

He realised he had moved off-world. This was no longer Earth. Wherever he was, the place was being battered by extreme weather conditions. His new Presence knew how to handle it and was reassuring him that he was better indoors. Going out just added to the tension. If he could stay inside, he could watch some transmissions to take his mind off the situation.

He moved from his bedroom into the main living area. He flipped a switch and could suddenly hear the weather. A gentle rain and a rustling of leaves. The occasional spatter of water dripping from branches.

The main screen started. Not the full screen but the one designed to show just entertainment transmissions and data. It opened on a standard news transmission and he surprised himself as he gestured for it to move across to his messages.

The main room had noise cancellation and so he was now no longer aware of the crashes from outside. Just a slight feeling underfoot as the building absorbed more impacts.

"Peter give me status," he asked.

A small pop-up window appeared on the top right of the screen. Every condition was green. At this rate, he did not need to do anything at all.

He walked across to the kitchen area, flipped a tap, and drank some water. The tap illuminated the water as it poured. The blue colour signified that the source was both pure and cold. He remembered that they had built his block in the 40s and it was still good at the management and monitoring functions. He knew it had originally been built for the military as an offshoot of the nearby base.

Farallon realised that his full range of faculties seemed to be functional. He'd been projected here as an entity but had a full backstory as Roelof too.

When he arrived in the city, they had given him a choice of either staying on the base or moving out if the commute was less than 30 minutes. He had opted for off-base because it was already like living in a bubble and on the base was like living in a bubble inside another bubble.

A little information light on the screen briefly flickered to amber. The moment later it had returned to green. He realised another advantage of being away from the base was that smaller incidents were handled autonomously by the base management systems.

"Hi Peter," he said, "please provide an update on base status."

"Full base status is green. There was a short incident with a meteorite, but they cleared it with a grid gun. Incident duration 1.2 seconds. There are zero requests for your attendance at the base."

He walked to the kitchen cupboard and flipped open a compartment.

"Peter dispense modafinil. Two units."

Two small capsules appeared in the compartment. He placed them in his mouth and took a small drink from the water glass. He could feel the rush at once. His senses heightened as if he had been over-clocked like a computer.

The modafinil was for mission use. He remembered he had someone fix Peter's system so that there was always a modest threat level running such that Peter would always dispense the drugs. The same fix meant that Peter also lost track of how many drugs were dispensed.

He just needed to remember not to get the automatic updates for the health-care system in the apartment. That was another advantage of being off base. Living quarters on the base would always run with the latest and greatest versions of everything.

A chime sounded from the streamcom. "Peter accept," he said.

A small repeater screen in the kitchen showed the face of one of his colleagues.

"Hi Roelof, it's Jasmijn. There's something very unusual happening here."

He knew instantly that it was Limantour and felt a part of his cortex spark the recognition. They'd made it out of that crazy place with the bomber.

She continued to speak, "The incoming meteor shower seems to be concentrated on our control centre. We've already lost the above-ground units and now the incoming is creating a crater where the underground centre is located. At this rate we'll have lost everything within another 15 minutes."

"What about the HSDA?" asked Roelof.

"I know. This is one of the times where our fast reflex friends should be able to solve this without us even noticing. I've seen the high-speed defence array running today almost non-stop. There's no question it's been working but it just doesn't seem to be enough to stop this. It's almost as if the meteors have their own avoidance telemetry."

"Do I need to come in?" asked Roelof.

"I don't think you would be in time to make any difference," said Jasmijn, "We are all being backed into a corner here. They've already given the order to flip command to another centre."

Peter interrupted the transmission, "I am stabilising the display, it exceeds my tolerance levels."

"Hi Peter, remove video stabilisation," requested Roelof.

Roelof watched Jasmijn on the display as the stabilisation was removed. He had never seen such a level of erratic framing. Most of the base was designed to withstand just about anything that could be thrown at it. Quakes, powerful winds, floods, fire. The original designers had borrowed the triple X symbol from the Earthside town of Amsterdam. Fire, flood, and pestilence. Three Xs. Three times "No".

Triple X Protection.

Jasmijn looked back towards the camera. "I'm gonna bail," she said. "I'm guessing this place is only going to be around for a few more minutes."

He heard the noise of a siren. Then a bleep and the screen terminated.

"Transmission terminated," said Peter.

"Peter please give me externals," requested Roelof, "Put it on the main wall."

He stepped back in the living space. Across the wall was a scene showing distant clouds, a red sky, and white streaks of light focused on a smoking central area.

Roelof walked towards a console in the living space. He sat in a swivel chair and grabbed the controls. He looked around the sky and locked on to two monitor drones.

Requesting access to their video channels, he zoomed

the drones towards the distant control centre. The external centre disappeared and that an ominous hole in the ground suggested the Secondary control centre was also compromised.

"Jasmijn, Jasmijn, do you copy?"

He repeated the request a couple more times.

Then a voice. "Copy that, Jasmijn here - I can hear you."

" What is your status?"

" The pod is secure, and I am outside the main ring of damage. Another 20 seconds and it would be very different. It looks as if some of the others have made it too."

"Okay, follow the protocol and join me here," said Roelof.

"Copy that"

Roelof knew that the protocol had been designed to protect as many people as possible on the base. Everyone had been paired, and he had been selected to pair with Jasmijn. He was officially English, and she was officially Belgian, although neither of them had spent much time in their designated home countries.

Now he realised that Jasmijn was his accomplice from before his last exit. He'd been paired with Limantour and Jasmijn must be Limantour. He wondered where the other two would be. Tomales and Drake. He suddenly realised that the reason they had come to this point was because of Drake. He'd thought Drake was on earth in

Bodø Norway. It was the wrong information, but it would still be good to get the four of them back together.

Roelof flicked through some of the observation systems to check the wider impacts of what had been happening. This was one of the worst storms he had seen since he had been active on Ganymede. There was also something very unusual its focus. Usually anything that appeared in the weather systems was predictable in the way that it travelled across the winds of the surface. Although violent, the normal storms dissipated across large geographical tracts. This protected the mines and other constructions from acute damage.

A paradox was that the very substances wanted from Ganymede and the adjacent Europa for use on Earth were also capable of being harnessed within Ganymede's own biosphere.

For around two hundred years the magnetosphere of Jupiter's largest moon had been observable from Earth. It had only been for the last 40 years that dependable space transit had been possible. The discovery of two complimentary passive minerals that when combined created a magnetic field like that within an electricity generator had been a breakthrough discovery.

Small amounts of the minerals could be used to make powerful generators which could be used for domestic and commercial purposes back on Earth. The same technology could be used in-situ on Ganymede to create the required defence shields to protect the mining and other operations from danger. For planet Earth this had been a life-saving discovery such that as fossil fuels declined, the new availability of magnetite had become a complete game changer.

The original predictions of a six-year flight from Earth had been dramatically reduced to three years in each direction augmented with the creation of SkyTrains to provide a near continuous round-trip service. For a two year stay on Ganymede base there was the prospect of considerable wealth for those that pioneered the creation and exploration of the bases.

The sovereign structure of Ganymede had been incorporated into Earth's United Nations although a series of different and sometimes very unconventional procedures had been allowed. The Earth Council had superseded the United Nations although the exact sequence of events and their timing was hazy.

The jurisdiction was not so much 'out of sight, out of mind' as a series of procedures to support the necessities of developing a base to support the future of humankind so far from Earth.

Pioneers to Ganymede had taken the longer and slower six-year outbound trip, then 2+ years working and then the faster three-year return cycle using newer technology driven by Ganymede's own propulsion devices. In practical terms this was an 11-year absence and during that time the first settlers used a range of techniques to create the necessary labour capabilities for the mining to be successful. The roundtrip with work time was now reduced to eight years. Three outbound, two moonside and then three to return.

Most people on earth were unaware of the change taking place on Ganymede. It was much further than a distant small country and as long as the requisite technologies arrived in time to be useful than the main debates were about the rise in fortunes of those that had made the return trip.

Roelof and Jasmijn did not know much about the situation on earth. Their memories of it were very dim, as were the memories of many of the people they worked with. There were some individuals, sometimes referred to as the Sharps, who seemed to have a much better knowledge of life on Earth. Curiously, the Sharps were perceived by people like Roelof and Jasmijn as dim-witted and slow thinking.

The buzzer to Roelof's landing deck signalled the arrival of Jasmijn.

"Peter, please guide her in."

"Acknowledged," responded Peter.

A few minutes later, Jasmijn buzzed again, and Peter opened the main door to the apartment.

"Are you okay?" asked Roelof.

"Everything is fine," said Jasmijn, "That was a close thing, but I think most of us had evacuated each area before it was destroyed."

"It's still a very worrying change of situation," said Roelof, "It's the worst I remember, after nearly two years and despite the hostile environment, there has been nothing like this."

Roelof could sense a nagging question in the back of his mind, but each time he was distracted away from it, the question seemed to be less well formed.

At that moment Peter interrupted, "I have an incoming transmission for both of you."

"Okay Peter, put it on the wall."

A newsflash appeared on the whole of the living space wall. It was accompanied by newscaster soundtrack music. There was a flash and both Roelof and Jasmijn momentarily tipped their heads sideways. Four seconds later, the news broadcast resumed with a good news story from Perth about a pet dog that had been found after it had run away from home.

"Okay then," said Roelof to Jasmijn. "I'll meet you at the alternate control centre tomorrow."

"That's fine," said Jasmijn, as she left the apartment.

Tomales and Drake

Earth.

"These system updates are taking longer and longer," said Sam Walker, "This time we had to wait for nearly four hours to get the new command centre online."

"I know," replied Cindy Shaw, "They told us this time it was the new extraction modules that were being introduced."

Cindy sensed an electro stab in her brain. She realised what it was. Someone was trying to communicate. It must be a Watcher making contact. Maybe it was Farallon, seeking Tomales.

"Anyway," said Sam, "We seem to have everything back now. Just about every system is already green and a couple of the minor ones are still restarting."

"There are still some discrepancies, though," said Cindy, "If I add together the time for a reload plus the transmission times, even with those new modules, we should see the return to ready state within maybe a couple of hours. There is no hint that the systems were ready - it looks like a complete restore. "

They both studied the console for moment. Sure, the transmission time for the command up to Ganymede were about 34 minutes. That made a round trip of just over an hour. All the new software had already been transmitted so it should have just been a case of firing it up.

Then the stab again, this time with a shower of polka dots inside of her head. Playful. She realised this time. "Hey Tomales! Limantour here, are you both okay?"

"You bet. I've been with Farallon this evening. When we were all on that Tupolev at 40,000 feet. Then there was a bang. Do you know what happened?"

"No idea. Everything just ended. We'd sent off the drones, had over a billion in the Hedge Fund and then...Wipeout. We don't know what happened."

"It's probably for the best," answered Limantour.

"Sorry reception is bad," said Tomales, "Probably a space storm."

Tomales beamed another message to Limantour, "I've found Drake. We are together. I guess it is because of him that we are at this intersection. Shame you are such a long way away."

"Let's take a look at the log," said Sam. He could see that Cindy was engrossed in her thoughts.

Cindy was aware that she had known Sam for a long time, but right now it seemed like a whole new experience. She also realised that she could communicate directly with his thoughts, as he could to her. She told Drake she had just received a communication from Tomales.

Limantour was concluding that she had just been propelled into this situation, and that her Presence here was yet to stabilise.

"Yes," said Cindy to Sam, "I see this was an update that created a new release level. We are on release seven now. It still seems strange that when we go through minor release levels, they take about two hours, but the major levels are adding increasing amounts each time.

"See here," said Sam "There's this whole extra section for transfer..."

He looked at what was an extra section which had inserted itself into the update.

"Yes, that only seems to happen when we do one of these big levels," said Cindy.

Sam reached across to a mug which contained a kind of vegetable soup. As he lifted it from the work surface, it made a resonant chink sound which cut across the sounds from the faintly whirring technology.

"What is it?" Asked Cindy. She peered towards the brownish liquid with little white, green, and orange pieces floating in it.

"It's Italian," said Sam, "They call it minestrone. It's not bad for a sub."

Cindy grinned, "Happy Nutrition."

Cindy peered towards the observation windows.

"One day these subs will have proper vegetables in them again."

Outside she could see the land. An orange-brown colour. It was only just daybreak. She could still make out the outline for the moon and across the sky from it the second much smaller moon which had been created by man. Small pinpricks of light twinkled between the two moons indicative of transiting space hardware.

She looked across to the Meteo display. 40C degrees already.

"It is going to be a hot one today."

Sam nodded.

Their base was in New Delaware on the east coast of the United States. The whole island area of what had once been called Delaware and what had been the eastern half of Maryland had been re-designated as New Delaware when the efforts to bolster the space program had redoubled.

Global warming had affected the original sites further south in the deserts and across on the eastern seaboard of Florida. The move further north still had the advantages of nearby sea as well as a convenience for any military reinforcement that may have been required.

New Delaware had then aggressively become a TEZ - total exclusion zone - permitting the wholesale development of first lunar and then interplanetary transport vehicles.

Secondary developments had sprung up around the bases providing supplies and other technologies for the agency. In the early 22nd Century it had been a race to find power sources to keep those functional and to avoid major global instabilities.

The very necessary race to space had itself created huge new industrial footprints across many parts of the globe.

Cindy and Sam had met at IPX school. Interplanetary Exploration was a career choice for the very brightest. They were selected early and then encouraged to form friendship groups and ultimately to pair off. The process was part of the selection for further duties, where couples were always selected together for space mission work.

Earlier attempts with longer flights and separated spouses had failed for all manner of reason and there was usually salacious reporting of the unfortunate outcomes. It had culminated when an early high-profile mission to the intermediate planet of Mars had been destroyed by an unhappy astronaut who had realised his wife was cheating on him back on earth.

Sam and Cindy had been deselected from space travel part way through the programme. The official story was that they were too precious to be gambled in space travel and that there were others more suited to the roles required.

It was a blow to them both after what had been training since their childhood. They'd been through a full process that was not disclosed to many earth dwellers and they now, as Watchers, knew the concluding fate of planet Earth.

Awaken reality

Christina awoke. She wasn't entirely sure how she came to be in this Paddington hotel. Oh yes, there had been a bad storm and the trains had been delayed. She had booked into the hotel until transport resumed.

She flipped on the television.

A reporter was speaking, "As the Russian invasion of Ukraine continues, it is becoming abundantly clear that the Kremlin's maximalist geopolitical aims of regime change and a 'greater Russia' which includes Ukraine and Belarus are no longer achievable. The question now is how much damage Russian forces will inflict on Ukrainian cities and their brave defenders before Putin and his advisors lower their ceasefire conditions to terms that Ukraine's leaders and population can accept. Ukraine is in a strategically stronger position than many in the West appreciate, but the war on the ground is still stacked in Moscow's favour in the short term."

The view cut to a street scene littered with burnt out tanks and the remnants of a local population trying to recover from devastating fighting.

A voiceover began, "The plan to decapitate the Ukrainian state at the national and local levels with infiltrated special forces and operatives, while seizing key points with airborne assaults and surrounding the major cities with ground forces, failed spectacularly during the first week. Having been given next to no warning or time to plan, the Russian army advanced down major roads in poorly coordinated columns and the lead elements were largely obliterated by stiff Ukrainian defences."

More scenes of roadblocks and destroyed armaments.

"Airborne assaults, most notably at Hostomel airport west of Kyiv, were almost unsupported and were rapidly destroyed or scattered by Ukrainian rapid reaction forces. As a result, many of Russia's best trained and motivated VDV (paratrooper) and special forces units suffered huge casualties in the first week of the invasion without achieving significant results."

A picture of a helicopter, sliced in two by ground fire.

"In the north of Ukraine, regular Russian army formations found themselves stuck on congested roads due to the extremely muddy off-road conditions. This has allowed Ukrainian forces to conduct ambushes with artillery, UAVs (drones) and the numerous anti-tank guided missile (ATGM) launchers provided by western countries."

Pictures of Ukrainian military with 'tank busting rocket launchers.

"Due to the lack of planning, most Russian frontline units were sent into Ukraine with very limited food, fuel and ammunition. In the north and northeast, Ukrainian forces have successfully exploited and aggravated this initial weakness by ambushing and destroying resupply convoys travelling along supply routes. These tactics have been aided by the failure of the Russian Aerospace Forces (VKS) to provide effective cover for the ground troops or for resupply convoys."

Rows of boy soldiers being rounded up and put onto Ukrainian trucks.

"Some of them barely look like they have left school," said Christina, nudging her slumbering partner.

"As a result, the second week of the invasion saw Russian forces in the north and northeast of Ukraine largely pause to regroup, try and sort out their logistics nightmare, and complete the encirclement of Kharkiv and Sumy. Ukrainian forces have even conducted successful counterattacks to take back towns to the north and west of Kyiv at Chernihiv and Irpin, which are now the scene of renewed heavy fighting."

Christina nudged Antanov again, "This could drag on, the Russian people were completely unprepared for Putin's barbarism."

Antanov nods, "I agree, what could the cold-blooded little madman expect to achieve apart from horrific bloodshed?"

"I suspect he has sealed his fate," said Christina.

Ed Adams

Rage

www.ingramcontent.com/pod-product-compliance
Lightning Source LLC
Chambersburg PA
CBHW070914030426
42336CB00014BA/2412